Digital Dollars

A step-by-step approach to making money while using social Media

Kunle R. Abisoye

Dedication

- To God who is the source all knowing and wisdom

- To my dear Sarah, Shammah, Shaun and Shalom, you rock my world

- To to my Parents, your seed continues to grow & thrive

- To all those who have taught and helped me, I say thank you

Contents

Understanding & Navigating the Digital Income Revolution

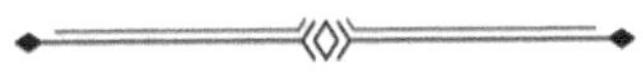

The advent of the digital age has brought about a seismic shift in the way we live, work, and conduct transactions. Much like the industrial revolutions of the past, this digital income revolution presents its own unique sets of challenges and opportunities. At the heart of this change lies an expansive realm where technology not only enhances productivity but also serves as a lucrative fountain of opportunity for income generation.

In exploring the landscape of this revolution, it is paramount to fathom the potential that this new era holds within its grasp. The digital world is not merely a collection of networks or gadgets, but a global marketplace where ingenuity meets opportunity, and where every individual has access to the tools needed to craft their financial destiny.

As we peel back the layers of this digital ecosystem, one can't help but marvel at the transformative power of social media, the internet, and cyberspace. These are the fertile grounds upon which fortunes are being made, sometimes with no more than a smart device and an internet connection. The diversity and accessibility these platforms offer exemplify the democratic nature of the digital economy—an open arena where the diligent and creative can flourish.

Amidst this dynamic environment, the potential for daily digital habits to become revenue-generating activities is often overlooked. This book aims to shed light on these hidden pockets of opportunity, revealing how everyday social interactions can be rethought and monetized. It's more than just about understanding these tools; it's about weaving through them with finesse and strategic acumen.

Esteemed reader, let's confront the stark reality: the possibility of generating substantial income digitally is no longer a distant mirage. Echoing through the pages that follow, you will find detailed, step-by-step strategies on realizing this potential. Whether your interest lies in creating content, leveraging social media platforms, or unraveling the intricacies of internet entrepreneurship, you will glean insights that can be actioned.

This guide navigates you through various digital revenue streams that are ripe for exploration. Making money digitally has never been more accessible; what it demands is developing a digital mindset attuned to wealth creation—a mindset that views every online interaction as a potential income source.

With each chapter meticulously designed, you will encounter those who have already scaled the heights of this digital domain, individuals from countless backgrounds who have reaped the rewards of an online presence. Their success stories serve not only as testaments to what's possible but also as inspirations for your own journey.

Anticipation may be mounting, and rightfully so. The digital domain waits for no one. Whether you're taken by sheer curiosity or a fervent resolve to act, the time is now to seize the day. Inaction can be the greatest inhibitor of potential; therefore, cultivating a sense of urgency and developing a personal action plan is critical.

Building your blueprint—a comprehensive strategy encompassing niche identification, audience engagement, and content monetization—is at the core of this book. Herein, practical steps are laid out to not only forge but also fortify your digital stakes. And as you embark on this journey, remember that each step forward, no matter how small, is progress towards a future where your digital endeavors can yield a thriving income.

Ultimately, as you navigate through this revolution, it is the learning, adapting, and continuous innovation that will set you apart. The digital income revolution is not just about embracing change; it's about being an active participant in shaping the trajectory of your financial future within this ever-evolving digital landscape.

CHAPTER 1

Digital Era - Uncovering the Income Earning Potentials of Today's Technology

In the fresh expanse of the digital era, where technology stretches its limitless horizon, lies a fertile plain for opportunities that can transform browsers into earners and socializers into financial opportunists. As we turn the page from mere understanding to actionable navigation of the Internet's vast potential, let's delve into the instruments that make this landscape a thriving global marketplace. Through the intricate webs interwoven within the framework of cyberspace, we find not just newsfeeds and networking, but a burgeoning ecosystem ripe for commerce, creativity, and ultimately, prosperity. It's an arena where ambition meets opportunity, and where the digital tools at our disposal serve as the keys to unlock monetary gains that were once thought to be the exclusive domain of the physical world. Embrace this transformative journey, as we explore how today's technology equips you with the power to craft your own financial destiny in a realm where the fertile ground of innovation continually yields new wealth.

The Internet: A Global Marketplace at Your Fingertips

Imagine the marketplace of old, bustling with traders from across lands, an emporium of endless possibilities. Now, conjure the concept of unlimited reach, the expanse of the globe interlaced at the click of a button, and you have the modern marvel that is the Internet: the quintessential global marketplace that resides within the grasp of your fingertips.

As we turn the pages of discovery, recognizing the potential held within the ethereal fibers of the Internet is vital. This digital space where transactions are not bound by physical limitations, the world truly becomes your oyster. Here, businesses can be initiated with lesser capital compared to their brick-and-mortar counterparts, and entrepreneurs can reach customers beyond their geographical confines.

The Internet is not just a conduit for commerce; it's a pulsating, alive ecosystem that interlinks creativity, innovation, and entrepreneurship. For those willing to lean into this digital windspeed, there lies a wealth of opportunities. You can craft an online storefront, offer services to a global clientele, and even market products that have yet to be invented.

Consider this digital realm as a landscape of opportunity. The traditional barriers to entry that have deterred many from starting a venture are significantly lowered here. A domain name, a hosting service, and a viable idea; these are the stepping stones to launching your digital shop. With such ease of setup, the Internet equalizes the playing field, making the dream of owning a business more accessible to many.

But how does one navigate this vast, seemingly infinite universe? The answer lies in understanding the consumer behaviors that dictate the flow of the digital economy. As you step into this realm, it's essential to grasp the nuanced dance between what the consumers desire and what the marketplace offers. Interconnectivity has provided consumers with the power of choice and their preferences, more than ever, shape the online landscape.

Marketing too has taken on a new avatar in this digital domain. It's no longer just about selling a product or a service. It's about telling a story, creating an experience, and building relationships. The Internet has enabled marketers to connect with their audiences in real-time, gather immediate feedback, and adapt with agility.

Furthermore, the global marketplace enables the forging of international partnerships with ease. Collaboration across continents is now as simple as a video call, opening up channels for innovation and cross-border entrepreneurship that were inconceivable in the past. Such collaborations can streamline operations, diversify product lines, and accelerate growth.

Data also plays an instrumental role in the grand theater of the global marketplace. Analytics can help predict trends, understand customer behavior, and tailor strategies to match. Armed with data, businesses can make informed decisions, refine their approach, and position themselves for success in the online ecosystem.

But an abundance of opportunity also brings an abundance of competition. As traditional geographical boundaries melt away, your competition isn't just the business down the street; it's also the enterprise across the ocean. To stand out, differentiation becomes key. Thus, identifying your unique value proposition is critical—it's the beacon that will guide customers to your digital doorstep.

Then there's the power of social proof in the Internet's marketplace, which can significantly amplify your business's reach and reputation. Reviews, testimonials, and social media mentions can create a compounding effect of credibility and visibility. This new currency of trust can be the difference between a one-time visitor and a lifelong customer.

The convergence of technology and commerce has resulted in groundbreaking platforms that facilitate online transactions. E-commerce giants, online payment processors, and digital marketing tools form the backbone of the contemporary marketplace. Leveraging these platforms efficiently can significantly reduce overhead costs and increase profit margins.

However, with such potential for reach and influence comes a heightened responsibility. Ethical business practices, customer privacy, and data protection are ever more paramount in the online space. As entrepreneurs and businesses, it's critical to adhere to the principles that foster trust and assure customers that their data is secure.

Thus, the global marketplace at your fingertips is not just an avenue for financial gain. It is a testament to human ingenuity, a celebration of global connectivity, and a reflection of our collective move towards an integrated economy. The responsibility to harness this realm with strategy, creativity, and integrity falls upon those who dare to step into the digital tide.

In closing this discourse on the global marketplace, let's embrace the wisdom that lies in this digital expanse. For as you learn to master the chords of the Internet's marionette, you'll find it's not merely about earning an income; it's about contributing to an ever-expanding digital civilization where each of us has the potential to thrive and shape the marketplace of tomorrow.

So, harness these insights, craft your digital strategies, and enter the marketplace with a clarified vision. The Internet awaits, not as a daunting challenger, but as a partner in the quest for innovation, success, and digital enlightenment. Here lies before you a canvas vast and receptive; may your venture leave an indelible mark in the annals of this global commercial odyssey.

The Social Media Landscape: More Than Just Likes and Shares

Social media has burgeoned into a vast ecosystem that far transcends the mere act of accruing likes and shares. It embodies a transformative platform where communication, creativity, and commerce collide in a digital dance of opportunity. Within these networks lies the potential not only for social engagement but also for significant income generation.

The anatomy of social media dictates a sprawling web of connections, each thread representing potential audience engagement, brand partnerships, and revenue streams. Here, every post, tweet, or story is a seed sown in the fertile ground of digital real estate. The fruit it bears, however, depends largely upon the strategies employed in nurturing these seeds. You are the digital gardener, and your harvest is the livelihood you can cultivate online.

Engagement in this context goes beyond mere digital nods of approval to encompass meaningful interactions that build communities and loyalty—assets that are invaluable in the digital marketplace. The astute entrepreneur recognizes the worth in each comment, message, and repost, leveraging these not just for brand visibility but also as insights that drive product development and market positioning.

Partnerships with brands have emerged as a key channel for monetization on social media. Content creators and influencers often curate a personal brand so compelling that larger corporate entities can't help but tap into their niche audiences. These symbiotic relationships fuse the clout of influencers with the resources of established brands, often leading to profitable endeavors for both parties.

Affiliate marketing is another frontier within the social domain, where your advocacy for a product can translate into a share of the profits. It requires a delicate balance of trust and tactical promotion—your recommendations must be genuine and verifiable, resonating as authentic endorsements rather than forced sales pitches to maintain credibility among your audience.

Beyond these collaborative efforts, social media enables direct sales channels through integrated storefronts and service promotions. The social savvy individual can effectively transform their profile into a dynamic storefront, capitalizing on the immediate engagement and reducing the friction typically associated with navigating to external sales pages.

Data, often regarded as the currency of the digital age, is particularly potent in the hands of those adept in social media analytics. Understanding metrics, from the reach of your posts to the demographics of your audience, equips you with the power to tailor your content and offers, thereby maximizing income potential.

Viral content is the holy grail of the social media realm—an Aladdin's lamp waiting to be rubbed. However, creating such content is less about chance and more about strategy. Recognizing trends, leveraging meme culture, and tapping into the zeitgeist are just a few tactics that can astronomically amplify your message's reach.

Content diversification across multiple platforms ensures a broader net is cast in the vast ocean of digital audiences. What resonates on Instagram may not have the same impact on Twitter. Thus, by diversifying, you mitigate the risk of changes in platform algorithms or shifting user preferences, assuring a steady stream of audience engagement, and by extension, revenue.

For those with an entrepreneurial spirit, social media is not just a space for expression but a launchpad for ventures. Crowdfunding campaigns, social media-driven startups, and the promotion of digital products and services all find fertile ground in the social ecosystem. It has become a springboard for ideation, validation, and support curation.

Subscription models and exclusive content offerings, enabled by platforms like Patreon, have introduced a revenue model based on recurring support rather than one-off transactions. This approach builds a sustainable income stream for creators committed to delivering value consistently to their patrons.

However, the richness of the social media landscape carries with it the need for digital literacy and a nuanced understanding of the platforms' inherent laws and etiquette. As sprawling as the digital space is, so too are the responsibilities it impresses upon its moneymakers. From copyright laws to platform-specific guidelines, it's imperative to navigate these waters with both ambition and prudence.

At its core, social media is a narrative medium. The stories you tell and the manner in which you weave them into the tapestry of the digital narrative will ultimately define your success in converting followers into customers, and likes and shares into dollars and cents.

As you stand at the precipice of possibility that social media represents, understand that your vision, voice, and value proposition are your currency. Invest them wisely and watch as your digital empire expands, underpinned by connections that are far deeper than the surface metrics of likes and shares.

Thus, the social media landscape is a cosmos of opportunity for those who dare to look beyond the superficial and understand the vast web of connections, innovation, and commerce it embodies. It's a place where creativity meets strategy, where engagement begets opportunity, and where the value delivered commands the income deserved.

CHAPTER 2

Equal Access, Equal Opportunity - The Democratic Nature of Digital Earnings

Embarking on a journey through the realm of digital earnings unveils a vital truth: the playing field is more level than ever before. In this world, your voice can be as influential as any, and your ideas can find an audience without the barriers of traditional gatekeepers. The internet does not distinguish based on geography, socioeconomic status, or education; it's a meritocracy rewarding creativity, value, and innovation. It's a place where a teenager in a remote village can conceivably earn as much as a seasoned executive in a bustling city, provided both have an internet connection and a strategy. This chapter explores how digital channels introduce unprecedented financial inclusion, allowing anyone with determination and access to technology to build a source of income. Here, we shall delve into the quintessential traits that make the cybersphere an egalitarian marketplace, and examine the essence of this equality, not as a distant ideal but as an attainable reality for millions pioneering their way into the digital economy.

Leveraging Technology for Financial Inclusion

As we transition from one chapter to the next, a vital conversation unfolds on the cusp of this digital frontier—financial inclusion. Technology, specifically the internet, has orchestrated a symphony of opportunities for millions to join the global marketplace. Our focus now turns to understanding how this digital crescendo is enabling a more inclusive economy.

Financial inclusion is the premise that individuals and businesses, regardless of their socioeconomic status, have access to useful and affordable financial products and services. These must be transactions that meet their needs, conducted in a responsible and sustainable way. The digital landscape stands as a testament to how technology can bridge traditional barriers.

Imagine a world where traditional banking obstacles, such as geographical distance and hefty bureaucratic requirements, dissolve into the digital ether. With technological advancements, particularly internet accessibility and smartphone penetration, people previously excluded from the financial ecosystem are now active participants. This is not merely a pipe dream, but a rapidly unfolding reality.

Online platforms and mobile technology have become powerful tools for financial empowerment. They enable a person sitting in a remote location to participate in economic activities that were previously out of reach. Emerging payment systems, mobile wallets, and online banking platforms facilitate transactions with convenience and speed, turning the tide towards financial democracy.

E-commerce platforms exemplify the power of technology in fostering financial inclusion. By providing online marketplaces, they offer individuals and small businesses the ability to sell products and services on a global scale. They shatter geographical limitations, allowing sellers to reach buyers thousands of miles away.

Social media stands alongside these platforms as a dynamic catalyst for financial engagement. It's not just a playground for personal expression and connection but also a fertile ground for entrepreneurial pursuits. Entrepreneurs leverage these networks to build businesses, create brands, and engage directly with consumers, which positions them squarely in the economic arena.

Collaborative finance frameworks, like peer-to-peer lending and crowdfunding, further illustrate technological strides towards inclusive finance. These platforms bypass traditional funding routes, offering entrepreneurs and individuals the chance to invest, loan, and fundraise within a more approachable and diverse financial community.

Education has also benefited from the march of technology towards inclusivity. Online resources, courses, and forums disseminate knowledge about financial literacy, legal considerations, and market trends, equipping individuals to make informed decisions and actively engage in the cyber economy with confidence.

Moreover, fintech innovations are tailoring financial services to suit unique consumer needs, fostering customization and inclusivity. These solutions range from microfinance to insurance technologies, wealth management tools to budgeting apps—all designed to integrate inclusive financial practices into everyday life.

The stories of success and transformation resonate profoundly. Entrepreneurs hailing from underserved communities, individuals with limited educational backgrounds, and those who have faced systemic financial exclusion, now recount tales of digital triumph.

The thread connecting these stories is technology's capacity to level the playing field.

For the youth exploring routes to economic success, technology-fueled financial inclusion brings more than hope. It delivers a platform for generation and dissemination of entrepreneurial ideas, fostering a vibrant community eager to capitalize on digital opportunities.

There is, however, a word of caution amidst this optimism. Not all that glitters in the digital domain is gold. Accessibility issues persist, and unequal internet access remains a significant hurdle. Therefore, continuous efforts are imperative to ensure that the digital divide does not widen but contracts, making the economy more inclusive for all.

As we delve into the exciting possibilities of financial inclusion via technology, we must also be mindful of safeguarding digital ethics. Transparency, privacy protection, and cybersecurity must be upheld to maintain the integrity of the inclusive digital financial ecosystem.

Concrete steps towards leveraging technology for financial inclusion are already underway. They present a clear blueprint for harnessing digital tools to create a more equitable economic landscape. Strategies such as digital training for the underserved, investment in internet infrastructure, and supportive regulatory frameworks are pivotal in this journey.

In closing the discussion on this fundamental topic, we recognize that technology isn't just a luxury afforded to the affluent. It's an essential catalyst driving us toward a future where financial barriers are no more, and the doors to economic participation are open wide. The horizon is broad, and the digital realm beckons with a promise of inclusion for all who are willing to embrace its potential.

Case Studies: Success Stories from Diverse Backgrounds

The journey through the landscapes of social media, the internet, and cyberspace for financial empowerment is as varied as the individuals who embark upon it. Success in this realm isn't restricted to a singular path or methodology; the tapestry of triumph is woven with diverse threads. Imagine scenes of vigor and tenacity, stories as varied as the colors of a kaleidoscope—each narrative serving as a guiding light for those who dare to dream and do.

In the heart of this digital revolution, we find a young coder from a remote village with limited access to resources. But within the confines of those four walls, dreams were not bound. With a relentless spirit, this individual mastered code through online courses and built mobile applications that solved everyday problems in his community. The revenue streamed in from app sales and in-app advertising, dramatically transforming his financial reality.

Consider the artist with an eye for beauty but a life graced with economic hardship. Social media platforms became her canvas, and her captivating illustrations resonated with an international audience. By sharing her journey and creating bespoke pieces, she built a loyal following which translated into a viable income through commissions, merchandise, and tutorial classes.

Encounter the story of a single parent who, amidst juggling responsibilities, discovered the power of affiliate marketing. With acute insight into the struggles and needs of others like her, she curated and recommended products that genuinely assisted her audience. Her authenticity earned trust, translating into steady clicks and purchases, and thus, a stable and growing income.

There's also the tale of a retired veteran who sought to give back by creating a community for fellow service members. His Facebook groups provided support and resources which soon attracted the attention of larger organizations seeking partnerships. Sponsored content and joint ventures became the norm, and his effort to serve others began to serve his own livelihood as well.

In every corner of the globe, from buzzing metropolises to tranquil towns, individuals are redefining what it means to earn a living. A mother in a small village crafts handmade goods and, through Instagram, her unique creations reach buyers far beyond her local market. Her sales skyrocket, and she's not just an artisan anymore; she's an international businesswoman.

Imagine a university student who leverages his love for gaming into an income-generating live stream on platforms like YouTube. His engaging commentary and strategic gameplay gather a plethora of viewers. Partnerships, sponsorships, and ad revenue transform his passion into a thriving venture.

Tales of teenagers reaching into the depths of the internet to emerge as cryptocurrency investors illustrate the audacity of youth and the possibilities of the digital age. They navigate this complex terrain with the acumen of seasoned traders, adapting to trends with swift precision.

Transitioning from traditional industry to the digital marketplace, a factory worker develops online courses sharing her in-depth knowledge of manufacturing essentials. Her wisdom, once confined to a factory floor, now empowers individuals across the globe, and her digital course sales create a significant additional income stream.

The awe-inspiring accounts of immigrants using language apps to learn new tongues and subsequently launching translation services online reveal how the barriers of language are not insurmountable. They not only reach financial stability but also forge seminal connections across cultures.

Then, there's the transformative story of a health enthusiast who uses WhatsApp to build a community focused on wellness. As her network grows, so does her influence, and she eventually monetizes through coaching services, digital meal plans, and fitness programs.

What can be gathered from these varied stories is a common vein of resilience, ingenuity, and the utilization of digital tools to unlock potential. From online marketplaces to networking platforms, each story underscores the vast opportunities awaiting those who are prepared to look, learn, and leap.

The fabric of success in the digital age is not restricted by age, background, or location. It celebrates the spectrum of human experience and the boundless potential of individuals willing to innovate and adapt. It's not always a straightforward journey—for many, it involves learning from failures, adjusting strategies, and tenaciously pursuing goals.

As these case studies demonstrate, the journey to digital financial success invites a panoramic range of participants. Each narrative is a compelling testament to the reach and inclusiveness of the digital era. They illuminate the vitality of social media, the internet, and cyberspace as a means to achieve not only financial prosperity but also to manifest personal missions and visions.

The trials, tribulations, and victories documented in these case studies serve as a beacon to those who are just beginning their quest or who may be facing doubt and uncertainty in their digital endeavors. Such success stories echo the truth that for those willing to grasp the digital reins and navigate through the cyber terrain, the possibilities are as vast as the horizon.

What must be taken away from these accounts is more than mere inspiration; it's a blueprint of possibility. Each story lays a brick on the path to potential that we all walk upon. They are proof that the digital income revolution is not exclusive—it's an unbiased landscape where determination, creativity, and grit stand as the currencies of advancement. This is the age where your unique story can be written into the annals of digital success—as long as you're willing to take the first step and keep striving for every subsequent one.

The Hidden Treasure Trove - Opportunities Missed on Social Media and the Internet

In our continuing exploration of the vast potential offered by our interconnected world, Chapter 3 delves into the underutilized riches of social media and the internet. Amidst the daily ritual of scrolling and interacting, many overlook the virtual goldmine at their fingertips. Each comment, post, and share holds untapped potential, not just for connecting with friends, but for generating revenue in ways that blend seamlessly with your digital habits. This chapter will illuminate the paths less traveled by the masses, where subtle shifts in the way we engage online can unlock profitable ventures. It will inspire you to see beyond the surface, to grasp the numerous possibilities that are hidden in plain sight, and to seize the opportunities that so many inadvertently pass by. As we shed light on these missed chances, you'll learn that each pixel of your screen can be a stepping stone towards a flourishing online presence and a more prosperous future.

Daily Digital Habits with Earning Potential

In the tapestry of today's interconnected society, our daily digital habits hold the power to not just inform and entertain, but to create streams of income that, with dedication and strategic execution, can often rival traditional earnings. It's within the seamless weaving of these habits where the genesis of a financially fruitful online venture lies latent. Every interaction, every search, and every post carries the potential of being transformed into a monetizable opportunity.

Consider the content you consume each morning; the blogs you read, the news websites you scour, and the newsletters that slide into your inbox. These are more than just morning rituals—they are the breeding ground for discovering niches that you are most passionate about, which can become your niche markets. By aligning your interests with those of others, you're positioning yourself to provide value—and where there is value, there's potential for profit.

Let's think about the social media platforms that pull us in for a light respite. Platforms such as Twitter, Facebook, or Pinterest are often viewed as distractions. Yet, these networks can serve as lucrative channels for building personal brands or promoting products and services. A single viral post, a well-curated board, or a consistent presence can attract advertising opportunities or sponsorships, turning routine interactions into revenue.

There are countless stories of individuals who've leveraged their daily screen time to achieve remarkable financial success. These aren't mere coincidences but results of deliberate actions and awareness of the power held within their digital habits. For instance, participating in forums and online communities, once seen as a leisure activity, is now a means to establish expertise, network, and eventually market your services.

Creative expression, too, holds an incredible earning potential within the digital domain. Writing, graphic design, video production—all of these are tasks often embarked upon for personal satisfaction or creative release. However, platforms like Medium, Dribbble, or YouTube provide the opportunity to convert these expressions into a source of income through advertisement sharing, sponsorships, and commissioned work.

It's pivotal to explore the daily digital tools that serve practical purposes—tools you likely use for organization or communication, such as Google Suite or Slack. These tools become powerful when leveraged correctly. For example, mastering these platforms can lead to opportunities such as becoming a virtual assistant, managing online businesses, or teaching others how to maximize the benefits of these tools through courses or webinars.

What about the time devoted to games or interactive entertainment? Indeed, such spaces have also morphed into avenues for income. The emergence of e-sports, online tournaments, and live streaming has opened the doors wide for gamers and enthusiasts to turn their dedication into dollars, whether through winning competitions or cultivating an audience that is willing to support their entertainment.

As we chart throughout the day, the digital habits of shopping and browsing e-commerce platforms can be transitioned into earning opportunities as well. By recognizing trends and consumer needs, one can establish dropshipping businesses, engage in retail arbitrage, or create and sell highly-demanded products on platforms like Etsy.

Your habitual engagement on social media platforms can go beyond idle scrolling. When you dive into the language of analytics or understand the algorithms, you can offer your skills as a social media strategist or consultant to businesses seeking to enhance their digital footprint, opening yet another revenue source.

Furthermore, the simple act of listening to music or podcasts during your daily routine can spark the illumination of pathways to income generation. By synthesizing what you learn or creating your own content to be shared on platforms such as Spotify or Apple Podcasts, you can establish a following and monetize your content through sponsors, affiliates, or premium content subscriptions.

Photography, once a hobby for cherished personal moments, now carries monetary potential thanks to websites like Shutterstock or Getty Images. Your daily captures, when uploaded to these platforms, can be sold to a global audience seeking quality imagery for personal or commercial use.

Email, the cornerstone of professional and personal communication, can turn into a profit center through the cultivation of a strong newsletter. By providing exclusive content, insights, or early access to products, you can convert a subscriber list into a source of sustained revenue through membership fees or the sale of specialized information products.

Don't neglect the role that daily learning and self-improvement habits play in this ecosystem. Online courses, certifications, and information products crafted from your accrued knowledge can be highly valuable to others also seeking to grow and learn.

Search engine queries, a habit as natural as breathing in the digital age, pose a unique opportunity. With SEO expertise, you can optimize content to drive traffic and monetize that traffic effectively through advertising, sponsorships, or affiliate marketing.

In conclusion, these daily digital habits in the modern age are rich with potential. By mindfully acknowledging each action's possibilities, you can slowly construct a diverse set of income streams that resonate with your lifestyle. It may begin with a single click or a post, but it can unfold into an unprecedented financial journey that honors the mosaic of your digital routine.

Rethinking Social Interactions for Profit

As we delve into the fabric of daily digital habits, it's crucial to shift our focus to a fundamental aspect of our online existence — our social interactions. For many, social media serves as a platform for personal expression and connectivity. Yet, in this evolving digital era, these interactions hold a well of untapped potential for monetary gain. Let's embark on a transformative journey, redefining our engagements in cyberspace to harness the power of profit.

Imagine your social media profiles as more than just platforms for sharing life highlights. Instead, every post, every connection, becomes part of a larger strategy serving your financial aspirations. This shift in perspective transforms passive scrolling into active networking, where each interaction is an investment in your digital portfolio.

Content creation is often perceived as an activity reserved for 'influencers.' Yet, the truth is that we all contribute to online content, and each contribution can be monetized. By creating value through relevant, engaging posts, you become a magnet for opportunities. This value attracts not only followers but also potential collaborators and sponsors who are willing to pay for your influence and expertise.

Engagement is the currency of the social media realm. Interacting with others through comments, shares, and messages builds relationships that can result in partnerships, affiliate opportunities, or client leads. Every interaction should be meaningful with the goal of adding value to another's experience—or subtly nuding them towards your own platforms and services.

To elevate social interactions for profit, cultivate a brand personality that resonates with your intended audience. Just as major companies have clear and compelling brand identities, so should you as an individual. This personal branding is not only authentic but also strategically constructed to align with the interests and needs of your audience.

Networking on social media opens doors to collaboration and mentorship. Joining groups and forums related to your niche fosters connections with like-minded individuals and potential mentors. These connections can lead to joint ventures or guidance that could exponentially accelerate your digital income journey.

Critical to this rethinking process is identifying the platforms that serve your goals best. Not every social network yields the same results for each individual or business venture. Allocate your energy where your audience thrives and where engagement aligns with your interests and skills.

Diversification is as vital online as it is with traditional investment portfolios. Your social media presence, like a well-balanced stock portfolio, should be spread across different platforms to amplify reach and reduce risks associated with algorithm changes or platform-specific issues.

Translating virtual engagements into real-world profits requires an understanding of the monetization tools at your disposal. Many social media platforms offer native means to generate income, from sponsored posts to ad revenue shares. Mastery of these tools can significantly increase your digital earnings.

Customer service and engagement often occur in the comment sections and direct messages of social platforms. Providing impeccable customer service not only boosts your credibility but also lays the groundwork for repeat business and referrals—which are as significant online as they are offline.

Consistency in online interactions builds trust and recognition. By keeping a regular presence on your chosen platforms, you create an expectation of reliability. This reliability translates into a dependable brand, which followers and consumers gravitate towards for their needs—and are willing to pay for.

Data analysis of your social interactions can guide you towards what works and what doesn't. Understanding metrics such as engagement rates and conversion statistics is essential to refining your strategy for profitability. Fine-tuning your online behavior based on data-driven insights is the hallmark of a successful digital entrepreneur.

Staying informed about the evolving landscape of social media and internet opportunities is non-negotiable. As new platforms emerge and old ones evolve, so too must your strategies. Stay agile and willing to learn, embracing changes that could lead to new avenues for profit.

Your digital footprint is more than what is seen on the surface; it's a web of interactions that, when leveraged thoughtfully, can lead to tremendous financial growth. Rethink your approach to social engagements not just as a means of communication but as a foundational element of your financial prosperity.

In conclusion, the paradigm of social interactions online is rapidly shifting towards monetization. With the right mindset, understanding of the tools, and a dynamic strategy, your everyday social media activities can become a lucrative business. It's more than simply being online—it's about being strategic in every digital move you make.

Digital Dollars - You Too Can Make Your Money Digitally

With the groundwork laid for the vast opportunities awaiting in the ever-expansive digital landscape, Chapter 4 ushers you into the transformative space of generating digital income, empowering you with knowledge to harness the financial streams flowing through the internet and social media. The intricacies of digital revenue are not just for the tech-savvy or the exceptionally creative; they're accessible to anyone willing to cultivate a mindset oriented toward digital abundance. In this chapter, you will navigate through the various pathways your digital quest can take, from content creation to strategic online engagement, all designed to manifest your monetary objectives. As we delve into the essence of a digital mindset for wealth creation, remember that your journey to financial prosperity is as unique as your fingerprints. Within these pages lies the fertile soil from which your digital dollars can bloom, provided you plant the seeds of disciplined action and nurture them with steadfast commitment.

Understanding Digital Revenue Streams

In the expansive terrain of digital opportunity, income generation is not merely a byproduct of fortuitous events but a deliberate march towards recognizing and harnessing the multifaceted streams of revenue that flow through the internet. As we navigate the vastness of this digital ecosystem, it is essential to demystify the variety of ways in which one can monetize online presence and content.

To truly grasp the possibilities, consider the diversity of platforms at your disposal. Each medium—from blogs to podcasts, from social networks to online marketplaces—serves as a conduit for financial gain. The challenge and, indeed, the opportunity, lies in identifying which streams align with your skills, passions, and available resources.

Advertising revenue remains among the most accessible streams for online entrepreneurs. Websites adorned with carefully placed ads generate income with each click or impression. Partnerships with ad networks can make this process seamless, offering content creators the ability to earn while focusing on their craft.

Subscription models present another avenue, turning a regular audience into a steady income stream. Whether through gated content or premium memberships, users pay for enhanced experiences or exclusive access, providing content creators with predictable revenue.

Affiliate marketing is a potent force in digital economics, allowing creators to earn by promoting products or services. When followers purchase through your affiliate links, a commission finds its way to your account, connecting your influence directly to your income.

Product sales open yet another profitable channel, empowering online personalities to sell digital or physical goods to their audience. E-commerce integration allows for smooth transitions from content to commerce, capturing the economic potential of your online influence.

Licensing and royalties provide content creators with passive income as their work is used or featured by others. Musicians, photographers, and software developers frequently benefit from this stream, as their creations continue to generate revenue with minimal ongoing effort.

Brand partnerships and sponsorships offer lucrative deals, where creators align with companies to promote products or services. With the right endorsements, creators can significantly increase their earning potential, marrying their personal brand to the value offered by partners.

Donations and crowdfunding harness the goodwill of an audience, enabling fans to directly support creators they appreciate. Platforms like Patreon exemplify this revenue model, allowing supporters to contribute financial assistance in exchange for various rewards.

Consulting and coaching harness your expertise, translating knowledge into revenue. By offering services directly related to your digital niche, you can monetize the skills and insights that have fueled your online success.

Speakers and workshop leaders find digital platforms to be an excellent source of income, as they offer webinars, courses, and speaking engagements to a global audience. The scalability of digital tools allows them to reach more people with less effort compared to traditional venues.

In-app purchases and gaming economies cater to the vast market of app users, providing digital goods or benefits within the framework of apps and games. Developers and content creators can profit from the in-game transactions made by their user base.

Lastly, content syndication and repurposing allow creators to maximize their efforts by distributing content across various platforms or modifying it to suit different mediums. This not only increases reach but also opens up additional income streams as content is monetized in various forms and locales.

But understanding these revenue streams is only the beginning. To convert knowledge into wealth, one must not only recognize the streams but also navigate them with precision and strategic acumen. Grasp the nuances of each channel and align them with your unique digital proposition. Learn to synthesize these streams, creating a robust and resilient portfolio that can withstand the ebbs and flows of the online world.

The empowerment that comes from mastering digital revenue streams is transformative. It eradicates the barriers of traditional employment, offering a canvas of potential limited only by one's creativity and drive. So harness this knowledge, apply it with diligence, and mold the digital landscape to reflect your vision of success.

Developing a Digital Mindset for Wealth Creation is fundamentally about internalizing a perspective that embraces the vast opportunities presented by the digital world. It's about understanding that the paths to financial success are no longer confined to traditional avenues. We're tasked with recognizing that the very fabric of commerce and profitability has been woven anew by the threads of technology.

In a realm where anyone can establish a global footprint from their living room, mindset is everything. Consider the internet a fertile ground, and the digital mindset a form of cultivation—a necessary preliminary to sow the seeds of online revenue. This mentality is about being agile, adaptive, and forward-thinking. It is also about cultivating a continuous learning cycle where one is always exploring new platforms and strategies.

Building this mindset starts with knowing the scope of digital possibilities. It's essential to stay informed on the latest trends in technology and online business. This knowledge empowers you to identify where opportunities lie and how they can be leveraged to your advantage. It's about harnessing the power of digital tools to broaden your entrepreneurial horizon.

Having this mindset also involves shedding the fear of failure; embracing the digital realm's trial-and-error nature. Surely, not every online venture will succeed, but each attempt is a learning experience—a stepping stone on the pathway to digital wealth creation. It's about resilience and the willingness to iterate and evolve.

One of the secrets of a digital mindset is networking and community building. In a space where algorithms and numbers often dominate discussions, human connections remain crucial. Wealth creation online is not a solo undertaking. It requires you to engage with others, learn from peers, and create value for a community.

Think of social media platforms not just as engagement tools, but as laboratories for testing ideas, receiving feedback, and forging partnerships that can lead to financial opportunities. It's about seeing every interaction as a potential lead or a spark for an idea that could translate into income.

Moreover, a digital mindset necessitates an understanding of the value exchange dynamics online. Your ability to monetize content hinges on the perceived value you offer to your audience. It demands a strategic approach to content creation, one that aligns with the interest and needs of your target demographic, and compellingly articulates the value proposition.

This mindset also encompasses the notion of scalability. Digital businesses have an unparalleled advantage in their ability to scale rapidly with relatively low incremental costs. As such, wealth creation in this context often involves creating systems, processes, and content that can scale without consistent manual effort.

Privacy and security are also integral to a digital mindset, particularly when dealing with financial transactions. Wisdom dictates a proactive approach to protecting one's digital assets, whether it's through secure payment gateways, data encryption, or regular audits and updates of security protocols.

Additionally, a digital mindset for wealth creation acknowledges the importance of diversification. Just as a knowledgeable investor diversifies their portfolio to mitigate risk, a digital entrepreneur should diversify their income streams to ensure stability and leverage different digital platforms to their advantage.

Embracing analytics and data plays a crucial role in this process too. In the digital space, numbers and metrics are the compasses that guide decision-making. They provide insight into what's working and what isn't, allowing for data-driven strategies that enhance profitability.

Moreover, a key element of a digital mindset is understanding the psychology of online behavior—why people click, share, and purchase. It's about crafting compelling narratives and calls to action that resonate with the digital audience's behavior patterns and expectations.

It's crucial to recognize that developing a digital mindset is a perpetual process. As technology evolves, so does the landscape of digital wealth creation. Being adaptable and staying informed are not just beneficial habits—they are essential to survival and success in the digital realm.

Lastly, developing a digital mindset means setting aside assumptions about who can be successful online. It's about embracing the democratizing power of the internet, which levels the playing field and allows anyone with determination and insight to create wealth. It rejects preconceived notions and stereotypes, often proving that creativity and innovation are boundless, not beholden to geography or background.

To sum it up, adopting a digital mindset for wealth creation is about more than just harnessing new tools—it's about embracing a culture of innovation, adopting a perspective of exploration, and cultivating an appetite for calculated risk. It requires you to be resourceful, reflective, and relentless in the pursuit of the opportunities that the digital landscape offers.

CHAPTER 5

Statistically Speaking - The People Making Millions Online

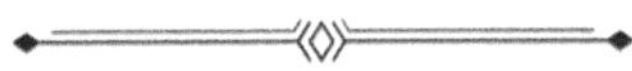

In previous chapters, we've explored the transformative potential of digital tools and platforms and shed light on the hidden opportunities that lie within our daily digital interactions. As we delve into the heart of this narrative, it's essential to ground our aspirations in empirical evidence. Within this chapter, we shall examine the statistical landscape, bearing witness to the awe-inspiring successes of intrepid individuals who're masterfully navigating the currents of cyberspace to accrue wealth. The evidence shows a clear surge in the number of entrepreneurs who have harnessed the connectivity of social media and the vastness of the internet not merely as tools for expression, but as fertile soil for the seeds of financial prosperity. These digital magnates come from all walks of life, breaking demographic barriers, and their triumphs are not just outliers; they symbolize a shifting paradigm, a testimony that the keys to the kingdom of online riches are within reach for those who dare to understand the metrics of success and align themselves with the principles that govern this new world of online enterprise.

Statistics of People Making Money Online Through Social Media and the Internet

In the digital currents of the 21st century, the Internet represents a vast sea of opportunity, glistening with potential for wealth creation. A diverse array of individuals have navigated these waters successfully, harnessing the power of social media and other online platforms to generate income. These individuals are not limited by geographical boundaries, nor confined by traditional job descriptions.

The statistics paint a compelling picture: a multitude of people from across the globe are accomplishing financial success online. And while the exact numbers ebb and flow with the tides of innovation and market demand, certain trends stand steadfast. Let's delve into some of these measurable indicators that reflect the state of digital earnings through social media, and what they signify for aspiring digital entrepreneurs.

Firstly, consider the rise of the influencer economy. A recent survey indicates there are millions of influencers across various platforms, with Instagram leading the pack. In fact, it's estimated that over a billion dollars are spent each year on Instagram influencers alone. The reach of these influencers varies, but even those with a smaller audience—so-called "micro-influencers"—can carve out lucrative niches.

Then there are content creators on YouTube who turn their viewership into a steady stream of revenue. The platform has paid out billions to its creators since the advent of its partnership program. Creators can earn through ad revenue, channel memberships, super chats, and more. The allure is evident: create engaging content and watch your bank account grow alongside your subscriber count.

Furthermore, the gig economy has blossomed on the web, with freelancers selling their skills online. Statistics from leading freelance platforms show that a significant portion of the workforce now freelances, with many citing increased earnings over traditional employment. From graphic designers to writers, a digital portfolio can become a magnet for global clients.

Diving deeper into specifics, there are those who leverage the affiliate marketing industry, which is worth billions. They earn commissions by promoting products through their social media channels or blogs. The appeal here is scalability: with the right strategy, one can continue to make money while sleeping, eating, or taking a leisurely walk through the park.

Alongside these individual successes, e-commerce continues to surge, with small businesses and solo entrepreneurs finding their markets online. With platforms like Shopify or WooCommerce, barriers to entry have been radically reduced. It's reported that in recent years, tens of billions of dollars have been processed through these platforms annually.

Moving to a realm less visible to the casual observer, there's the burgeoning space of online course creators and educational content. E-learning platforms have experienced a dramatic increase in instructors, with revenue mirroring this uptick. Those with expertise in a particular field can reach students worldwide, turning knowledge into income.

Let us not overlook the phenomena of social selling and direct sales. Leveraging the power of personal networks, thousands are making money through the social media sales of products and services. This is not the door-to-door sales of the past; it is digital, it is direct, and it is decentralized.

Moreover, a considerable percentage of online income is generated through the development and sale of digital products, such as software, apps, music, books, and other media. This sector is teeming with creators and developers, whose inventiveness finds an enthusiastic and ever-growing audience online.

When we aggregate the numbers globally, we see that hundreds of millions of people are engaging in some form of digital work. Not all are witnessing monumental success, but many are finding sustainable, profitable avenues. It's a broad spectrum, ranging from full-time incomes to supplementary earnings that enhance financial stability.

Increasingly, we're also witnessing the rise of social commerce, where traditional social networking and e-commerce blend. As this phenomenon grows, a growing number of social media platforms are incorporating buy-buttons, shops, and other commercial features that allow users to make instant purchases. Analysts predict that social commerce sales could reach into the hundreds of billions in the next few years.

These statistics, while illuminating the scope of online income generation, only scratch the surface. They hint at a more profound narrative: the democratization of opportunity. The digital age has enabled the enterprising spirit to flourish, unencumbered by many of the constraints that once stifled innovation and commerce.

Equipped with this insight, it's clear that there's a transformation afoot—a shift toward an economy where initiative, creativity, and connection are the currency of the realm. As we consider these numbers, we see not just statistics, but stories of individual courage, ambition, and achievement.

In summary, the evidence is overwhelming—making money online isn't just possible; it's becoming a part of the new norm. To dismiss these stats is to ignore the tidal wave of change that is reshaping how we work and live. Arm yourself with this knowledge, and let it fuel your journey in the boundless digital marketplace.

So while the figures will continue to evolve, the lesson they teach us remains consistent: the Internet offers a fertile ground for those willing to sow the seeds of their hard work, creativity, and innovation. Integral to your success is understanding the importance of positioning oneself strategically within this vast and varied online ecosystem.

As we sail into the next chapter, armed with statistics and the stories they tell, let us focus on harnessing these insights. It's time to plot your course in the digital landscape, shaping your own narrative within this growing community of online earners.

Analysis: What the Numbers Say About Digital Success

Diving into the numerical heartbeat of digital earnings uncovers a plethora of insights. Analytics tracks the footsteps of every successful online venture. From view counts to engagement rates, these metrics hold the compass that guides us through the topography of digital success. Within this realm, statistics not only demonstrate who is amassing wealth online but also reveal how they're doing so.

The significance of user engagement cannot be understated. Consider the average percentage of followers who actively interact with content; these figures often translate directly to the potential reach of a product or personal brand. Digital success is thereby not measured by followers alone but by the quality and depth of these relationships.

Monetization strategies also paint a picture when we analyze the numbers. Video creators, for instance, often see a direct correlation between watch time and revenue. Data speaks to the efficiency of different monetization channels, as well, whether it be through ad revenue, sponsored content, or direct sales. Each method's efficacy is etched clearly in the numbers.

Conversion rates shine a light on the potency of a digital strategy. Understanding this data equips us with the necessary insights to refine our approach. High conversion rates are emblematic of resonant messaging and well-targeted campaigns, crucial elements in attaining digital prosperity. These rates are the benchmarks against which all online income initiatives must be gauged.

Moreover, it's not merely about quantity but the quality of traffic that determines digital fortune. Insights into demographics offer a trove of data, suggesting whether content aligns with the intended audience. The granular detail of analytics allows one to tailor strategies to specific age groups, geographic locations, and interests, thereby maximizing relevance and, in turn, income potential.

The escalation of digital revenue follows an upward trend as more individuals tap into the internet's potential. A survey of who is making money online reveals a wide array of profiles, each exploiting a unique avenue within the digital landscape. The versatility of online platforms underscores the myriad ways in which one can achieve monetary success.

Recurrent patterns seen in successful online entrepreneurs are illuminative; high-earning individuals and businesses exhibit consistency in content creation and audience engagement. The frequency of updates seems to have a proportional relationship with a successful digital footprint, suggesting that persistence is as important as the content itself.

The applied analysis of return on investment (ROI) underscores the effectiveness of digital spend compared to traditional forms of marketing and sales. The numbers argue in favor of digital realms where lower overheads align with potentially higher returns. A careful study of ROI statistics can steer investments toward more profitable digital practices.

Time spent on different platforms offers its own tale. The emerging dominance of mobile usage, for example, sheds light on shifting behavioral patterns and the importance of optimizing for mobile devices to capture mobile-first audiences. Those who harness this information can ride the wave of mobile trends to commercial success.

Revenue generated across various online platforms defines the current hierarchy of digital income. Such financial statistics lend critical insight into platform popularity and effectiveness. They inform us where time annd resources might be most beneficial ly invested to yield the highest returns.

Customer retention metrics also serve as strong indicators of sustainable digital success. A one-time purchase pales in comparison to repeat business. Again, the number tells the story: Brands that invest in customer satisfaction and loyalty programs often see recurrent earnings and maintain a steadfast online income stream.

Lastly, the upward trajectory of e-commerce signals that buying and selling goods and services online is no temporary trend. E-commerce growth statistics forecast a fertile ground for those who aspire to carve out digital revenue streams in the marketplaces of the internet.

Gleaning from the number-driven narratives, we see that digital success is not just about being online; it's about strategic, informed movements within an ever-burgeoning cyberspace. Those who grasp the numerical language of digital platforms can decode the secrets to financial gains and reap the benefits of a well-executed digital strategy.

While metrics can guide, they too require prudent interpretation. It's the synthesis of quantitative data with qualitative insights that fosters a robust online presence and successful digital income stream. Pairing statistics with human insight bridges the gap between numbers and narrative, illuminating a path to digital success.

In synthesizing these metrics with one's individual goals, an actionable blueprint for digital earnings emerges. For those embarking or currently navigating this journey, understanding what the numbers say about digital success is an indispensable part of the process. Each statistic tells a story, and when heeded, can lead to profitable outcomes in the diverse and dynamic landscape of the digital income revolution.

CHAPTER 6

Time to Capitalize - Stop Waiting, Take Advantage

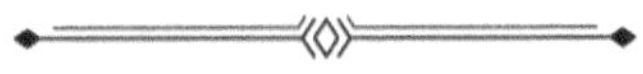

Amidst a universe of opportunities that the digital sphere unveils, hesitation becomes the harbinger of lost potential. This chapter stands as an unequivocal call to action—a persuasive pledge that underscores the exigency of seizing the digital day. It is in this juncture of our journey that the line between contemplation and realization must be crossed. Recognizing that the inertia of procrastination and the crippling grasp of analysis paralysis only serve to undermine the wealth of prospects at your disposal, we must foster an invigorating sense of urgency. There exists a dynamism in the artistry of time—momentum to be harnessed by those willing to act with prompt resolve. As we delve deeper, we dispel the misconceptions that delay is prudent, situating ourselves in the fertile grounds where proactivity intertwines with strategy; where we consciously craft a personal action plan that aligns with the fluid rhythms of cyberspace commerce. Now is the appointed time to capitalize, to take advantage of the boundless banquet of digital possibility set before us. Let us navigate these waters with decisive strokes, for the tide of opportunity awaits no one.

Overcoming Procrastination and Analysis Paralysis

As we pivot to the vital task of proactive execution in the realm of digital earnings, it becomes essential to address the common impediments that stifle action: procrastination and analysis paralysis. Both are formidable adversaries in the pursuit of success, yet they are not insurmountable. To combat these obstacles, one must first understand their nature and origins.

Procrastination, the thief of time, often arises from a misjudgment of one's abilities or an overestimation of the time available. Analysis paralysis, meanwhile, is the result of an overwhelming barrage of options or excessive data that stalls decision-making. In the fast-paced digital landscape, where opportunities emerge and dissolve with astonishing speed, succumbing to these pitfalls can mean missed fortunes.

The initial step in overcoming these challenges is to establish a mindset refined for decisive action. This involves recognizing that perfection is an illusory goal and that the pursuit of excellence can proceed alongside action. Accept that mistakes are an integral part of the learning process and that every misstep is a stepping stone toward greater understanding and eventual success.

Commence with the understanding that clarity often comes from engagement, not thought. While it's essential to strategize, it is equally critical to transition quickly from planning to doing. Begin with small, manageable tasks to break the inertia of inactivity. The key is to start — once momentum is gained, it becomes easier to maintain productivity.

Organize your tasks by priority and tackle them one at a time, focusing on the critical activities that will advance your goals significantly. This is known as the Pareto Principle, or the 80/20 rule, where roughly 80% of the effects come from 20% of the causes. Applied to digital entrepreneurship, this means honing in on the select few strategies and actions that yield substantial results.

Set deadlines for yourself, even if arbitrary, to provide a sense of urgency. Parkinson's Law states that work expands to fill the time available for its completion. By restricting the time you allocate to a particular task, you encourage efficiency and thwart procrastination.

Take advantage of technology to automate or simplify decision-making where possible. Use scheduling tools, reminders, and productivity apps to keep you on track. These tools can free up mental space and reduce the burden of choice, making it easier to proceed with critical actions that generate income.

Surround yourself with a support system—an assembly of peers, mentors, and like-minded individuals who can offer accountability and encouragement. Being part of a community committed to growth and action can powerfully counteract the forces of procrastination and analysis paralysis.

Visualize success and maintain a clear vision of your goals. Visualization is not mere daydreaming; it is a potent tool that primes your mind and body to recognize and enact the steps necessary to achieve your objectives. Place visual reminders, such as vision boards or goal lists, in your workspace to keep your targets at the forefront of your mind.

Remember that flexibility is pivotal. The digital landscape is ever-changing, and a strategy that might be fruitful today could become redundant tomorrow. Develop a flexible mindset that embraces adaptability and is willing to pivot when necessary. This practice will allow you to make decisions more quickly, knowing that you can adjust your course if the situation demands.

Develop a set of guiding principles or a personal framework for making decisions. This helps reduce uncertainty by providing a consistent basis upon which to evaluate options. For example, prioritize actions that align with your core values, contribute to your long-term vision, or have a proven track record of success in your field.

If you find yourself mired in analysis, impose a 'five-second rule' — if you're unable to make a decision about an action within five seconds, simply choose the path that feels most aligned with your goals and commit to it. Decisiveness fosters confidence, which in turn fuels further action.

Recognize that in the digital age, timing is often everything. Aligning action with opportunity can be the difference between success and stagnation. As you engage more deeply with digital platforms and strategies, you will start to develop an intuition for the right moments to act. Trust in that intuition as much as the data at your disposal.

Finally, adopt a philosophy of continuous learning. When you commit to learning from each experience, whether it ends in triumph or in lessons learned, there is no true failure. Every action taken is an investment in your education as a digital entrepreneur, which over time, accrues to significant intellectual wealth.

As we delve into the subsequent chapters, particularly the creation of a personal action plan and identifying your niche, remember that these strategies for overcoming procrastination and analysis paralysis are to be revisited and refined. They are not merely tools to begin your journey but companions to aid you throughout the persistent climb to digital profitability and success.

Creating a Personal Action Plan

As you embark on a journey to harness the digital landscape for income, it's essential to inscribe your aspirations in a well-crafted action plan. This plan will serve as your roadmap, transforming lofty visions into executable strategies. A detailed action plan is not merely guidance; it is the catalyst to actualize what you've learned thus far about earning digitally through social media and the internet.

The foundation of your personal action plan starts with setting clear, attainable goals. Begin with the end in mind, envisioning where you wish to be in this digital income revolution. Establishing your desired outcomes will focus your efforts and provide motivation when you face inevitable obstacles. Goals should be precise and measurable, with established timelines to keep you accountable.

After goal-setting, it's imperative to assess your current skills and resources. Evaluate what you already possess that can aid you in your online ventures, and identify what additional skills or resources you'll need to acquire. Personal growth is a continuous process, so align your learning path with your goals, prioritizing those competencies that will bring you closer to digital earning success.

A thorough understanding of your niche and target audience, as discussed in later chapters, is vital, but you should begin pondering this now. Reflect on your passions, expertise, and the market demand. An action plan that marries your interests with a niche in need is more sustainable and fulfilling. You're more likely to persist when the work aligns with your intrinsic motivations.

Now, consider the platforms you'll leverage. Each social media network and online marketplace has unique features and audiences. Which platform aligns best with your goals and the content you wish to create? Your action plan should detail not only your platform of choice but also how you'll use its specific tools to your advantage.

Your action plan must include a strategy for content creation. Content is the currency of the digital world, so plan what you'll create, how often, and what value it will provide your audience. Ensure the content strategy aligns with your brand and message, and remember that quality trumps quantity.

Financial planning cannot be overlooked in your action plan. Detail your expected revenue streams, consider initial investments, and anticipate potential expenses. Having a clear financial projection will help you stay disciplined with your spending and gauge the success of your digital efforts.

Networking and collaboration are key components of a robust action plan. Identify individuals or groups within your niche who can be mentors, collaborators, or part of your support network. Plan how you'll connect with these vital contacts and the mutually beneficial relationships you aim to build.

Mindset is as crucial as mechanics. A portion of your plan should be dedicated to fostering a positive and resilient mindset. How will you maintain motivation, handle setbacks, and sustain mental well-being? Define your support system and stress-management techniques to sustain your drive and focus.

Accountability is critical to staying on course. Outline how you'll track progress, be it through a mentor, a mastermind group, or self-reflection. Decide on regular intervals to review your objectives, celebrate wins, and adjust your course as necessary. Make accountability a non-negotiable part of your journey.

Risk assessment is another essential factor in your action plan. Consider potential pitfalls and have contingency plans in place. Risk management will enable you to respond swiftly in adversity without derailing your entire digital income strategy.

With a comprehensive action plan, you're ready to implement and take consistent action. Break down your larger goals into daily, weekly, and monthly tasks. This breakdown transforms your plan into manageable steps, preventing overwhelm and promoting steady progress.

Adaptability should be woven into the very fabric of your action plan. The digital landscape is ever-evolving, and flexibility will be one of your strongest assets. Schedule in time to learn, adjust, and evolve your strategies as new information and opportunities arise.

Remember, success is not solely about what you do but also about who you become in the process. Your action plan should help mould you into an individual that epitomizes discipline, creativity, and perseverance. Embark on this digital earning endeavor not just to make money, but to grow and leave an indelible mark on the world.

May your action plan be the steady pulse guiding your digital income aspirations, and may your journey be filled with growth, discovery, and success. With each day comes a new opportunity to advance your mission, so grasp each moment with conviction and an unwavering determination to realize your digital potential.

CHAPTER 7

Building Your Blueprint - Practical Steps to Fortify Your Digital Stakes

Embarking on this venture, it's essential to marshal the resolve and clarity of vision that lie at the heart of great undertakings. This chapter is your forge, where we turn raw ambition into a structured plan. Here, you'll learn the craftsmanship required to establish a robust online identity, grounded in the authenticity of your niche. Cultivating a digital presence isn't a mere task; it's an art form that requires careful articulation and strategic finesse. To truly succeed in the digital terrain, you must embrace the disciplined practice of shaping an online persona that resonates with your intended audience—those who seek the unique value you provide. It's a matter of identifying the intersection where your passions meet the market's needs. Step by confident step, this chapter guides you in the crafting of a foundation so steadfast that your digital stakes become not only visible but formidable, leaving an indelible mark in the virtual sands of your chosen domain.

Identifying Your Niche and Audience Online

The concept of niche and audience identification stands as a cornerstone in the blueprint of your digital enterprise. As we embark on this journey, it's imperative to underline the significance of precision and clarity when pinpointing the specific sector within the vast marketplace that aligns seamlessly with your passion and expertise. Your niche is more than a category; it's a reflection of your unique insights, values, and the distinctive voice you bring to the virtual congregation.

In a realm as colossal as the internet, your voice must resonate with a well-defined group of individuals — your audience. These are not just mere spectators in your digital odyssey; rather, they are collaborators and co-creators of the community you aspire to build. Their interests, challenges, and aspirations should harmonize with the content and solutions you provide.

So how does one thrive in recognizing these crucial components? Initially, it requires introspection. Probe into your personal and professional experiences. What subjects spark your enthusiasm? Where do you possess a wealth of knowledge or a unique perspective? Is there an underserved segment that you can illuminate with your vision? Answering these questions is a formative step in sculpting your digital identity.

Following this self-examination, the emphasis shifts towards research. Delve into forums, social media discussions, and trend analyses. These digital societal fabrics are imbued with the desires and gaps felt by potential audiences. Seek out recurring themes and pain points that align with your discovered niche, providing a map that guides you to the heart of your audience's world.

It's crucial to grasp the concept that your audience is not a static entity. Understanding their evolving nature demands active listening and engagement. Pay attention to the shifts in their conversations, the news items that affect them, and the emerging trends. Every change in the digital pulse is a potential opportunity or warning signal for you to adapt and stay relevant.

As you unfurl the tapestry of your audience, it's pivotal to segment them accurately. Different subsets may have varying needs, and a one-size-fits-all approach is seldom effective. Tailor your communication to address specific subgroups, ensuring that each feels seen and heard. This creates depth in your relationships and fosters robust loyalty.

Remember the power of analytics in this equation. The data from your website, social media platforms, and online interactions can offer insights into who is engaged with your content and why. Utilize metrics to fine-tune your understanding and to continually refine your strategies. This analytical edge will serve as a compass for your digital endeavours.

The artistry in this defining process is not entirely strategic; it is also empathetic. Immerse yourself in the values and worldview of your identified audience. By adopting an empathetic mindset, you can create content that not only educates or entertains but truly connects with the hearts and minds of those you aim to inspire.

Building upon this foundation, you must then articulate your unique selling proposition (USP). What makes your digital offerings distinctive? Whether it's a novel approach, unparalleled convenience, or a transformative idea — ensure that your USP resonates unmistakably with your niche and audience. This singular narrative will become the beacon that magnetizes your community.

Your digital presence and offerings must intrinsically align with the preferred platforms of your niche audience. Certain demographics might gravitate towards visual mediums like Instagram, while others seek the communal discussions on

Facebook or LinkedIn. Choosing the right platforms is like setting up your shop at the busiest intersection of your target market's town square.

Engagement is the currency of the online world, and fostering a robust dialogue with your audience is indispensable. It's more than just a strategy; it's about building a communal table where ideas thrive, support is abundant, and everyone has a seat. Your audience should feel invested in your journey because through engagement, they contribute to the narrative of a shared future.

Throughout this iterative process of identifying your niche and audience, it's paramount to remain flexible and dynamic. The digital landscape is ever-changing, and agility in responding to new information and trends will allow you to pivot and grow in ways that are congruent with the evolution of your audience and advances in technology.

Lastly, document your findings and insights as you distill your niche and define your audience. Creating a living document that captures the personas and characteristics of your target market will act as a reference and guide for all your digital initiatives. It will inform your content creation, marketing strategies, and product development, contributing to a coherent and compelling brand experience.

Venturing into the realm of digital income is akin to embarking on a voyage across uncharted waters. By having a keen sense of direction and a deep understanding of the stars you're navigating by — your niche and audience — you become the capable captain of your own digital destiny. Embrace this endeavor with the bold assurance that the path you're carving online is not just about profits; it's about impact, community, and the relentless pursuit of excellence in the digital age.

With these insights and strategies, you're primed to not just identify but also to engage and grow with your niche and audience online. This is more than a mere step; it's the writing of an epic where you're both the author and the hero. The following chapters will continue to build upon this foundation, weaving together the processes and insights that will propel you towards a thriving digital income.

Constructing a Solid Online Presence is a fundamental pillar in the architecture of digital success. The concrete reinforcement of your digital persona aligns directly with opportunities found within the spaces of social media and cyberspace at large. With intention and finesse, constructing such a presence is not an overnight occurrence but rather a careful cultivation of content, connections, and credibility.

To begin with, your online persona must be a reflection of both your aspirations and the authentic core of who you are. Authenticity in the digital realm is akin to a beacon; it draws individuals to your energy and fosters trust—a currency of invaluable worth in an era where many are seeking to connect with genuine voices. Ensure your brand's voice remains consistent, for it will become the signature others come to recognize and depend upon.

Content stands as the cornerstone of your online presence. To emerge from the vast sea of digital noise, your content must be compelling, valuable, and tailored to the audience you aim to serve. Curating or creating content should not only demonstrate your expertise but should also resonate with the needs and desires of those you wish to influence or serve. Every post, article, or story you share should add a building block to the edifice of your digital identity.

Strategic engagement is another vital structure in your online presence. Active participation in conversations, timely responses to comments, and fostering dialogue are digital age equivalents to handshakes, smiles, and direct conversations. It's essential to not only talk but to listen actively, engage with empathy, and nurture relationships that could burgeon into partnerships or a loyal following.

Consistency in your online activities cannot be overstated. It's the frequency of your posts and interactions that will keep you at the forefront of minds and algorithms alike. However, this does not counsel for quantity over quality. Rather, it's the regularity of quality touchpoints that establishes a pattern of reliability and expectancy from your audience.

A visual identity adds another dimension to your presence. The psychology of color, imagery, and design plays a pivotal role in how your brand is perceived. Conscientiously design your visual collateral to align with the ethos and essence of your brand, ensuring it tells the story you want conveyed at a mere glance.

Optimizing profiles across platforms is a technical necessity. Utilize keywords, descriptions, and visuals that not only stand out but also are discoverable via search engines and internal search features. Your biography or about sections are not to be neglected; they are concise pitches to visitors that can convert a curious click into a dedicated follower or customer.

Thought leadership and subject matter expertise reinforce your structure of influence. By producing educational content that addresses your audience's pain points, and offering innovative insights, you cement yourself not just as another voice, but as a go-to resource in your field.

Collaborations and networking are akin to branching out with more arms to reach wider audiences. Connecting with other influencers and businesses in complementary or similar niches can amplify your presence through shared audiences. This synergy can lead to growth opportunities that may not have been possible in isolation.

Analytics and insights offer a back-end view to the efficacy of your online efforts. Utilize these tools to understand what content resonates, at what times your audience is most active, and from what sources your traffic originates. This data-driven approach enables you to optimize your strategies and grow your online presence with precision.

Crisis management is also a crucial consideration. Crafting a solid online presence also involves preparing for potential setbacks or public criticism. Develop a plan to address concerns transparently and constructively, turning challenges into opportunities for demonstrating integrity and commitment to your audience's trust.

Security measures are imperative, as the trust you build can be quickly eroded by cyber threats or data breaches. Protect your presence by utilizing strong passwords, two-factor authentication, and being vigilant about what you share online, ensuring that your digital presence is secure and your audience's data is safe.

Accessing the pulse of current events and trends keeps your digital presence relevant and dynamic. Integrating timely and topical content can position you as a current and engaged brand, adapting and evolving in accord with the world around you.

Feedback loops are essential for evolution. Solicit and value the feedback from your audience. Utilize surveys, polls, and direct communication to understand how your presence is perceived and where it can be improved. This creates a collaborative environment where your audience feels heard and valued, strengthening their investment in your brand.

Personal development should never be neglected—your growth as an individual directly influences the growth of your online presence. Keep learning, adapting, and staying abreast of best practices in the ever-changing digital landscape. Invest in courses, attend webinars, and read widely to ensure that your strategies remain cutting edge.

Finally, perseverance is the binding material in your construction process. Building a solid online presence requires patience, resilience, and dedication. Stay the course, refine your strategies, and remain focused on your vision. The digital realm is vast, but by anchoring your presence with depth and meaning, you create a space for others to find guidance, inspiration, and value— an enduring legacy in the digital income revolution.

CHAPTER 8

Monetizing X - Leveraging a New Platform for Income

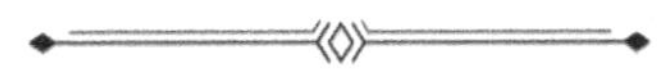

In the vigor of our digital odyssey, Chapter 8 imparts the discerning exploration of 'Monetizing X': a newly ionized platform suffused with prolific potential for those seeking to construct a stream of income as boundless as the cyberspace itself. We delve into its fabric, uncovering the tactics that transform innovation into income, and guide you through the strategic navigation of this platform, ensuring that you not only grip the helm but also chart a course towards the ultimate treasure of digital monetization. We survey the wisdom of those who have already charted these waters, distilling their case strategies into a potion of success ready for you to imbibe. Illuminate your path with the principles contained in these pages, for they are the spark that sets ablaze the beacon of entrepreneurship within the realm of 'X', affirming yet again that the digital landscape is fertile ground for those willing to sow the seeds of purpose and cultivate them with relentless action.

Navigating X for Maximum Profit requires an astute blend of strategy and persistence. As you venture into this space, it's imperative to understand the dynamics of X, a platform that's ripe with opportunity, yet laden with challenges that test even the most resilient of entrepreneurs. The path to profitability is not linear, but a rigorous understanding of X's mechanics can tremendously increase your likelihood for success.

In the realm of X, distinguishing yourself is paramount. Start with meticulous market research to gauge the demand for your product or service. Are there gaps you can fill? What unique value can you provide that isn't already oversaturated? Knowing this landscape is akin to understanding the currents before setting sail—you need to know where the waves will take you and how to navigate them to reach your desired destination.

Develop a compelling value proposition. What sets your offering apart on X? Is it exceptional customer service, unparalleled quality, or perhaps a revolutionary invention? Your value proposition should resonate with your target audience and be evident in every interaction and transaction on the platform.

Once your value is defined, it's time to engage with the community on X. Authentic engagement builds trust and credibility, two cornerstones of successful digital ventures. Foster relationships by providing insights, being responsive, and showing genuine interest in the needs and wants of your potential customers. Remember, in the digital marketplace connection often precedes transaction.

Pricing strategy on X should never be an afterthought. It's a critical component that requires a delicate balance: price too high, and you risk alienating potential customers; price too low, and you devalue your offering. Conduct competitive analysis, understand the financial demographics of your audience, and position your pricing in a way that reflects the value while remaining accessible.

Educate yourself on the technical aspects of X. What tools and features does the platform offer to maximize your visibility and sales? Could you leverage analytics to understand your audience better? A successful navigator not only sails the ship but also knows every rope and sail at their disposal.

Content creation on X isn't merely about quantity. High-quality, valuable content is the currency of attention in the digital economy. Align your content strategy with what your audience seeks, and make sure it's optimized for X's algorithms. This is how visibility converts to profitability.

Looking to the tactical side of navigation, timing is everything. When are your potential customers most active on X? What kind of content do they interact with at specific times during the day or week? Strategic posting can boost your content's performance, multiplying its impact on your profitability.

Maintaining scalable systems is crucial. As your following and customer base grow, so too should your capacity to manage increased demand. Utilize the tools available to automate where possible without sacrificing the personal touch that users of X appreciate. Preparation for scaling is a strategic investment in your profitability.

Risk management also plays a key role in navigating X. Diversify your offerings to safeguard against market fluctuations. Don't put all your eggs in one basket—examine various revenue streams available on X and determine which combination aligns best with your goals.

On the subject of goals, they should be as dynamic as the platform of X itself. Set clear, measurable objectives and be ready to pivot as market conditions change. What works today may not work tomorrow, and agility in your goal-setting ensures you remain on the path to profit.

Advertising on X should be targeted and well-conceived. A one-size-fits-all approach is not tenable in a diverse digital ecosystem. Craft personalized campaigns based on user data, test different ad formats, and invest in the ones that bring a significant return on investment.

Look beyond immediate profit and towards sustainable growth. Build a brand on X that's synonymous with quality and reliability. As much as quick wins are celebrated, enduring success is crafted through consistent excellence and a reputation that attracts repeat business and referrals.

Keep abreast of changes on X. The platform will evolve, and your strategies should be fluid enough to adapt. Stay informed of policy changes, new features, and shifting user habits. An informed navigator is better equipped to capitalize on change rather than being capsized by it.

In conclusion, navigating X for maximum profit necessitates a confluence of skillful planning and adaptability. Lay a robust foundation, conduct continuous learning, connect authentically, and stay future-focused to bring your vision to fruitful reality. Let your journey on X be etched with smart, strategic moves that secure your digital prosperity.

Case Strategies: Successful Entrepreneurs on X

Learning from those who have navigated the complexities of digital income can illuminate the path for new entrepreneurs. The platform we refer to as 'X' exemplifies innovation and adaptability, necessitating a diverse array of strategies for actualizing its monetary potential. To distill this wisdom, we delve into the experiences of successful entrepreneurs who have cultivated wealth through X.

Entrepreneurs understand that X's potential lies in its real-time connectivity and thriving community. A case in point is John, who specializes in niche marketing. John capitalized on X's capacity to create tightly-knit user groups around specific interests. His strategy involved fostering substantial engagement within these groups, which led to targeted advertising opportunities and direct consumer feedback, resulting in a robust revenue model centered on community-based marketing.

Another entrepreneur, Lily, leveraged the analytics tools provided by X to refine her marketing campaigns. By diligently examining data patterns, she optimized her advertisements to reach peak performance. This data-driven approach not only cut down on wasted ad spend but also significantly increased the conversion rate, yielding a higher return on investment.

Cross-platform integration is a strategy that Alex swears by. By seamlessly integrating X with other social media platforms, he was able to expand his reach and drive traffic towards monetized content. Alex's grasp of the interconnected nature of digital platforms led to a synergistic effect that magnified his online presence and earnings.

Mia, on the other hand, found success through influencer collaborations. By partnering with well-established figures on X, she gained access to wider audiences and presented her brand's narrative through authentic storytelling. This cultivated trust and loyalty among potential customers, translating to an increase in sales.

Pivotal to these strategies is content optimization. Richard, a content creator, focused on understanding the algorithm of X to ensure that his content gained maximum visibility. His posts are meticulously crafted to align with trending topics and user preferences, which in return, has attracted sponsorship deals and advertising revenue.

Digital services are another avenue explored on X. Sarah's consultancy business thrived by providing value through webinars and online courses on the platform. The live interaction feature of X allowed her to engage with clients in real time, offering a personalized service that set her apart from competitors.

E-commerce integration with X has been revolutionary for Emma. By embedding her online store within the platform, she created a seamless shopping experience for her customers. Emma's integration strategy has led to higher sales conversions and an uptick in repeat customers due to the convenience of in-platform transactions.

Raising capital through X is a strategy James found effective. By presenting his startup ideas within entrepreneurial circles on X, he attracted investors interested in leveraging digital ventures. This approach not only secured him necessary funding but also built a community of supporters for his brand.

An advertising approach was harnessed by Olivia, who utilized paid advertising on X to its fullest potential. With a keen eye on cost-per-click and audience targeting, Olivia's ads reached the right demographics, resulting in high engagement and securing a strong customer base for her product line.

Subscription models on X have worked exceptionally well for Nathan. By offering exclusive content and personalized experiences to subscribers, he created a steady income stream that grew monthly. Nathan's emphasis on providing value led to low churn rates and high customer satisfaction.

Monica's venture reflects the power of partnerships. By connecting with other businesses on the platform, she accessed new markets and leveraged cross-promotion strategies, effectively expanding her digital footprint while sharing resources and splitting costs with partners.

Community management is an area where Angelo excelled. By establishing and nurturing online communities on X, he created an ecosystem where participants actively engaged with his brand and each other, laying the groundwork for a self-sustaining hub of activity that drove sales through organic advocacy.

Sponsorship deals became a strategic revenue source for Zoe, who established her brand as an influential entity on X. By cultivating a robust follower base and demonstrating engagement metrics, she attracted sponsors eager to tap into her audience demographic, thereby establishing a lucrative sponsorship stream.

Focusing on mobile optimization is another key strategy. Since X is predominantly accessed via mobile devices, Daniel ensured his content and services were mobile-friendly. This not only amplified user experience but also spiked user interaction and conversion rates through ease of access and user interface design.

In conclusion, the entrepreneurial journey on X requires a combination of innovative strategies, adaptability, and relentless focus on creating value. The aforementioned strategies are just a snapshot of the ingenuity applied by successful entrepreneurs on the platform. With the right approach, X can be a fertile ground for digital income, offering a plethora of mechanisms for revenue generation – each requiring its unique formula for success.

CHAPTER 9

Instagram Income - Visuals That Generate Revenue

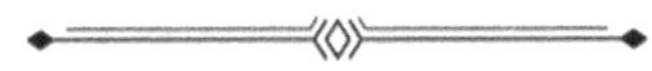

In the dynamic realm of Instagram, mastering the art of monetization is akin to understanding a visual language—a language where every image, video, and story you share holds the potential to unlock streams of revenue. The essence of commercial triumph on this platform lies within the craft of weaving captivating visuals with strategic intent. As an entrepreneur seeking to harness Instagram for financial gain, envision your content as a curated gallery, where each post must resonate with your audience's aspirations and inspire action. You're not just posting pictures; you're choreographing a visual symphony that speaks directly to the core desires and needs of your followers, transforming passive viewers into active customers. It's here, in this confluence of aesthetic allure and persuasive storytelling, that prosperity is painted in bold strokes of engagement and sales. By leveraging Instagram's unique tools to amplify your message, you'll not only capture the attention of your audience but also translate their interest into a sustainable income.

Crafting Content That Sells is not just an art; it's a strategic maneuver that requires an understanding of the heartbeats of the market and the tools to leave an impact. In a digital landscape that's saturated with messages, the content that sells is the one that stands out, not merely in being seen but in resonating with the audience. It understands the nuances of human desires and tailors its message to meet them where they are.

At the core of crafting content that sells is the principle of value. To generate content that sells, one must first have a profound comprehension of what the audience values. This understanding forms the foundation of all content—whether it's informative, entertaining, or motivational. It addresses a need or solves a problem. Your content must not only attract but also retain the audience's attention, urging them on a journey from interest to action.

Value, however, is not a static concept. It's dynamic, evolving with the landscape of desire and necessity. To keep your finger on the pulse of what sells, you must be both an observer and a participant. Observation will give you insight into current trends and effective strategies, while participation will grant you firsthand experience of what works and what doesn't.

Authenticity is the key to creating a connection with your audience. In a world where trust is currency, selling without sincerity is a shortsighted strategy doomed to fail. Your content should mirror the essence of your brand and the truth of your message. It's about creating a narrative that people can believe in, relate to, and want to be a part of.

Storytelling is a powerful tool when crafting content—it transforms features into feelings and statistics into stories. A well-told story has the power to engage the mind and the emotions, creating a memorable experience for the audience. Human brains are naturally wired to respond to stories, which makes narrative a crucial element of content that sells.

It's also critical to speak the language of your audience. If you're addressing tech enthusiasts, then a more sophisticated vocabulary might be appropriate. If your audience is younger, your content should be more energetic and relatable. This doesn't mean you sacrifice depth; it means you translate complexity into a dialog that's accessible.

Visually appealing content is not just an option; it's a necessity. In the realm of platforms like Instagram, where crafting content that sells is paramount, visuals are often the first point of contact with your audience. They not only attract but also communicate and represent your brand. Therefore, investing in high-quality, captivating visuals is an investment in the marketability of your content.

However, visuals alone won't suffice if the copy doesn't captivate. Words wield power, and the right ones can move markets. When paired with striking visuals, compelling copy can make your content not just seen but remembered. It can persuade, inspire action, and elicit responses that pure images cannot.

Call-to-action (CTA) isn't just a button or a line at the end of a post; it's a pivotal point in the content journey. Your CTA should be clear, compelling, and conspicuous. It should beckon the reader into taking the next step, whether that's to subscribe, buy, or simply learn more. Without a strong CTA, even the most engaging content may fall short in converting interest into action.

To effectively craft content that sells, one must also understand the power of timing and trend. This means knowing when to publish what content. It's recognizing the opportune moments that align with cultural moods or seasonal demands. Content released at the right moment can ride the wave of relevancy and garner significant traction.

Engagement must not be an afterthought. You must always encourage and be prepared for interaction because today's online platforms are more about dialogue than monologue. Crafting content that sells means being ready to engage, respond, and interact with your audience. It's about building a community around your content, a community that feels heard and valued, and which, in turn, values your message.

Data and analytics are indispensable tools. Evaluate what content performs well and adapt your strategy accordingly. Tools and resources are readily available to measure such metrics, and they provide invaluable insights into the mind of your consumer. By employing analytics, you're able to tailor your content to sell more effectively.

Consistency in content creation should not be compromised. Random spurts of content can't compete with a consistent narrative that builds and maintains momentum. Your audience should anticipate your content with the surety that it will be delivered as expected, reinforcing trust and establishing a reliable presence in a sea of unpredictability.

Finally, the mastery of crafting content that sells involves continuous learning and adaptation. Be bold in experimenting with new formats and platforms. Take risks, learn from them, and evolve. What sold yesterday may not sell tomorrow, and so your content must be as fluid and adaptable as the trends that shape the market.

The art of crafting content that sells requires aligning value, authenticity, and strategy in a seamless dance that captivates and converts. It's not merely about getting seen; it's about impacting lives, inciting action, and creating a narrative that the world doesn't just observe but wants to be a part of. As you hone this art, remember that at the other end of every post, every video, every image, is a person seeking an answer, a story, or an inspiration—make sure your content is the beacon that guides them.

Utilizing Instagram Tools to Boost Your Earnings

As we navigate the contours of Instagram, we uncover an array of tools designed to enhance our visual storytelling. These are not mere embellishments on a social platform; they are potent instruments that, when wielded with precision, can amplify our message and bolster our earning potential. The first step is unlocking the power of Instagram's analytics, affectionately termed Insights.

Instagram Insights serves as a beacon, illuminating the preferences of our audience. By studying metrics such as reach, impressions, and engagement, we gain vital knowledge of which content resonates most. We learn the days and times our followers are most active, allowing us to optimize our posting schedule, thus maximizing visibility and interaction. This data, if analyzed with a critical eye, can lead to a more strategic approach and consequently, a more lucrative outcome.

In a digital era where the ephemeral has taken center stage, Instagram Stories has emerged as a frontier for creativity and monetization. Stories engage because they are fleeting; they compel action because they are urgent. By integrating features such as polls, questions, and swipe-up links (for those with a following that meets Instagram's criteria), we invite direct participation from our audience, creating a two-way dialogue that increases engagement and fosters a sense of community around our brand.

Beyond the sphere of the transient lies the continuously evolving landscape of IGTV and Reels. Here, the opportunity to craft deeper, more immersive content awaits. IGTV caters to long-form video, enabling us to share comprehensive content that may educate, entertain, and inspire, leading to longer viewing times and increased loyalty. In contrast, Reels allows us to tap into the cultural zeitgeist with short, impactful videos that have the potential to go viral. Both avenues offer the advantage of discoverability through the Explore page, putting our content in front of new eyes and expanding our reach.

Utilizing shopping features on Instagram can turn our profile into a digital storefront. By tagging products in our posts and stories, we offer our audience a seamless shopping experience. With Instagram checkout, the entirety of the buying process—from discovery to transaction—takes place within the app. This convenience can drive sales and transform our profile from a mere showcase into a revenue-generating powerhouse.

Collaboration tools on Instagram present a symbiotic pathway to growth. Engaging with peers through features like co-branded content or Instagram's Collaborative Posts can introduce us to new audiences. By uniting with other creators or brands, we weave our narrative into a larger tapestry, adding depth to our story and expanding our reach.

Advertising on Instagram is undoubtedly a tool with tremendous potential. Whether opting for sponsored posts or stories, Instagram ads allow precise targeting, ensuring that our message reaches those most likely to be interested in our offering. A well-crafted advertisement, aligned with the interests and behaviors of our target audience, can be an effective investment, driving engagement, and elevating our earning potential.

Hashtags serve as signposts, guiding users to our content amidst a vast social landscape. Employing relevant and trending hashtags can catapult our posts to the forefront of conversations, making them more discoverable to those outside our immediate following. This strategy, when applied judiciously, can increase our content's reach and by extension, our profile's profitability.

An often-overlooked tool within Instagram is the power of direct messaging (DMs). While broadcasting content publicly is the norm, personalized interaction in DMs can build stronger relationships. By interacting directly with our followers or potential collaborators, we personalize the social experience, fostering trust and loyalty which are critical for converting followers into customers or partners.

Lastly, the virtue of consistency cannot be overstressed. While not a tool in the traditional sense, consistency in posting quality content establishes trust and expectancy among our followers. As our digital tapestry unfolds, each post contributes to an overarching narrative. Consistency keeps followers engaged, helping maintain visibility and relevance in a platform driven by algorithms favoring active, engaging content creators.

In harnessing these tools, it's not just about what we create, but how we deliver it. The discerning use of filters and editing tools can enhance the aesthetics of our content, making it more appealing and shareable. However, authenticity should never be sacrificed at the altar of perfection; our audience craves genuineness, and they can spot the inauthentic, which can tarnish trust and hurt our brand.

Moreover, interactive features such as Instagram Live offer us a stage to showcase our brand in real-time, inviting our audience into our world. Live sessions create immediacy and serve as a platform for announcements, Q&A sessions, and behind-the-scenes glimpses, building intimacy with our audience which can translate into increased earnings through heightened loyalty and engagement.

We must not underestimate the power of performance analysis. By regularly reviewing the performance of our posts and stories through Instagram Insights, we learn what works and what doesn't. This perpetual cycle of analyzing, learning, and optimizing is vital to a sustainable and profitable online presence.

Engagement is a two-way street. It's not enough to simply produce compelling content; we must also interact with our audience. By responding to comments, acknowledging feedback, and participating in conversations, we foster an engaged community, which is an invaluable asset in sustaining and growing our digital income.

In conclusion, Instagram is more than a collection of images and videos. It is a sophisticated suite of tools that, when used with intention and intelligence, can elevate our digital presence and enhance our earning prospects. Each feature offered by Instagram can be thought of as a brushstroke in the masterpiece of our online hustle. It's incumbent upon us to embrace these tools with the artistry and acumen they deserve, crafting a social media narrative that not only captivates but converts and sustains profitability.

CHAPTER 10

Facebook Fortunes - Connecting and Earning

As we forge ahead from embarking on visual storytelling that entices sales on Instagram, it is now time to delve into the vast ecosystem of Facebook—a platform teeming with opportunities ripe for the taking. Within this digital bazaar, the potential to cultivate wealth is bolstered by the sheer magnitude of global connections. Here, fostering relationships transcends beyond mere social interactions; it paves the way for building a business empire grounded on the principles of community and shared interests. This chapter elucidates how to monetize your presence on Facebook through innovative strategies that leverage the nuanced subtleties of the platform. You'll learn not just to engage but to enchant: transforming every like, comment, and share into stepping stones towards financial prosperity. Through a lens of intentionality and tactical precision, 'Facebook Fortunes: Connecting and Earning' offers you the blueprint to transition from passive socializer to an astute digital entrepreneur, guiding you on your journey to harvest the untapped wealth within your network and embody the spirit of a true cyberspace titan. Thus, let's embark on this transformative exploration of systematic monetization, where your venture into Facebook becomes a testament to your tenacity in commanding the digital space for robust earnings.

Strategies for Monetization on Facebook

In the quest to turn our Facebook presence into a stream of income, it is imperative to approach this platform with strategic intent and innovative action. Facebook, as a robust social network, presents an array of opportunities ripe for monetization. One begins by understanding the structure of Facebook's monetization capabilities, grasping the array of tools at one's disposal for generating revenue.

To harness the monetary potential of Facebook, we must anchor our strategy in content. Content creation is the crux of engagement; it lures the audience in with value, information, or entertainment. Crafting compelling content that resonates with your target audience establishes a solid foundation upon which monetization efforts can efficiently be built.

Further, a step into monetization on Facebook is to dive into the world of Facebook Ads. Advertisements offer the chance to not only expand one's reach but also to target specific demographics with precision, thus promoting products or services to those most likely to engage or purchase. Ad usage must, however, come with careful planning—devising budgets, analyzing metrics, and constantly tweaking campaigns for optimal performance.

Fostering a vibrant community is pivotal in monetizing a Facebook presence. Pages and groups that encourage interaction become hubs of activity, loyalty, and, ultimately, revenue, as engaged communities are more receptive to marketed products or services. Building a community demands authenticity and consistency, as it is the bridge that connects personal brands to their audience.

Affiliate marketing emerges as a powerful tool when we examine Facebook monetization strategies. By partnering with companies and promoting their products on your Facebook page, you can earn commissions on clicks or sales. This symbiotic relationship benefits both content creators and product vendors, provided the marketed items align with the interests and needs of one's followers.

The introduction of Facebook Marketplace has opened yet another avenue to generate income, providing a space to sell goods directly within the platform. Whether it's handcrafted goods, second-hand items, or digital products, Marketplace offers a streamlined process to reach buyers and conduct transactions.

Facebook Pages can be monetized not only through the sale of products but also by hosting sponsored content. Collaborating with brands to produce and share content tailored to your audience can lead to lucrative partnerships. Transparency and relevance are vital to maintain trust with your audience while engaging in such partnerships.

Subscriptions are increasingly becoming a standard, allowing creators to earn recurring revenue from Facebook's fan subscription feature. By cultivating a subscriber base that pays for exclusive content, you create a predictable income stream that can stabilize and grow your financial gains on the platform.

Another innovative strategy is to offer online courses or workshops through your Facebook page. Leveraging educational content positions you as an authority in your field and adds educational value to your followers while providing an income stream through course fees.

Live broadcasting on Facebook also opens up monetization possibilities. Facebook Live can attract a donated income stream through the platform's 'Stars' feature, where followers can offer financial support directly during a broadcast. Moreover, live events present an opportunity for real-time engagement and marketing of products or services.

Exclusive events and experiences also offer potential for monetization. By utilizing Facebook's event creation tools, you can host virtual events, charge admission, and provide unique experiences that followers are willing to pay for, like private Q&A sessions, virtual meet-and-greets, or specialized content.

In-game purchases and rewards have also been integrated into the Facebook ecosystem. If you're a game developer or a gamer, you can monetize your gameplay through in-app purchases offered to the gaming community on Facebook.

Optimizing the platform's shopping feature can significantly boost sales for those with tangible or digital products. Setting up a Facebook shop creates a seamless shopping experience, integrating e-commerce directly within the social media context. This convenience can enhance buyer willingness and increase transaction volume.

It is also worth considering the collection of donations for a charitable cause. By aligning your brand with a mission that resonates with your audience, you can raise funds through Facebook's fundraising tools, building community and goodwill while supporting worthwhile initiatives.

Lastly, the integration of the Facebook Instant Articles feature presents a way for publishers to create fast, interactive articles that can monetize through embedded ads. This feature not only optimizes user experience but also offers a new revenue stream for content creators.

In sum, monetizing your Facebook presence demands creativity, community engagement, and a savvy use of the platform's numerous features. Embrace the uniqueness of your brand, and use it to craft a monetization strategy that speaks authentically to your audience while providing value. The harmonizing of passion and strategic execution is what transforms a Facebook page from a mere social space into a bountiful digital storefront.

Engagement Techniques That Lead to Profit

In the realm of Facebook, an ocean of possibility lies within the dynamic framework of engagement. To turn engagement into profit is to master the art of conversation, community, and connection. This skilled navigation pivots not merely on chance but on deliberate and meaningful interactions.

Understanding that every comment, like, share, and message bears the potential for profit invites a strategic approach to online engagement. One must begin by cultivating a community around authenticity and trust. A page or profile imbued with these elements fosters a loyal following, inclined to advocate and patronize. To this end, ensure every piece of content shared, every response made, echoes with sincerity and offers value that resonates with the audience.

Utilizing Facebook's rich analytics tools allows for the strategic targeting of content. Insightful data breaks down the demographic and behavioural patterns of your audience. By leveraging this intelligence, one can tailor content and interactions to specific segments, increasing relevance, and subsequently, engagement rates which are a precursor to profit.

User-generated content bears the twin gifts of authenticity and endorsement. Motivate your followers to contribute content – be it through testimonials, reviews, or creative spin-offs of your products or services. Their content broadcasts to their networks, effectively magnifying your reach and enhancing trust among peers.

Consistency in interaction forms the bedrock of engagement. By establishing a regular posting schedule and promptly replying to comments and messages, one fosters a space where audience anticipation meets brand reliability. This consistency not only sustains current follower interest but also draws new eyes, widening the circle of potential conversions.

Promotions and contests on Facebook can ignite engagement in explosive bursts. Construct these with clear objectives, valuing quality interactions over mere quantity. Offer incentives that require participation beyond the superficial click - perhaps through content creation, or by sharing personal stories related to your brand. This depth of engagement seeds long-term relationships, which translate to increased customer lifetime value.

Live features on Facebook, such as live videos and events, offer unique avenues for real-time interaction. Here, the immediacy of the experience heightens engagement, as followers partake in an event as it unfolds. This strategy solicits comments and reactions at a rate higher than non-live content, resulting in greater visibility in newsfeeds - a direct line to enhanced profit potential.

Collaborations with influencers and other brands can expand your reach and add credibility through association. Choose partners aligned with your values and whose followers overlap with your target demographic. By crafting joint campaigns or events, one can tap into the trust that these influencers have cultivated with their followers, thus amplifying the likelihood of engagement and conversion.

Loyalty programs within Facebook encourage recurring engagements. By rewarding repeat interactions & purchases, you incentivize a continuous relationship rather than one-off transactions. Such programs can be orchestrated through point systems, exclusive content, or members-only groups – each fostering an elite sense of community that thrives on exclusivity.

Feedback mechanisms, such as surveys or an invitation for comments, turn engagement into a two-way street of conversation. This openness to audience input demonstrates a commitment to improvement and an appreciation for the follower's voice. Moreover, it supplies invaluable data that can refine marketing strategies and optimize future profit margins.

Through storytelling, a brand transcends the mundane and weaves a narrative that can captivate an audience. Harness the power of your brand's story across your Facebook presence. Such narratives foster an emotional connection, transforming passive followers into engaged storytellers and advocates of your brand themselves.

Education and value-add content distinguish a brand as an industry thought leader. Share tips, tutorials, and insights that empower your audience. As they derive tangible value from your content, their propensity to invest in your offerings climbs, leading to increased sales and profits.

In the pay-to-play landscape of Facebook, strategic investment in paid promotions and ads can also boost engagement, and therefore profitability. However, the secret lies not in the expenditure but the execution — targeting the right audiences with compelling and optimized creatives that resonate on a personal level.

Personalization elevates engagement from general broadcast to individual dialogue. Employing tools that allow for personalization, such as custom messenger bots, personalized video messages, or targeted content, can show each member of your community that they are more than just a number. This personalized approach can lead to enhanced trust and loyalty, which bolsters the prospects of turning engagement into tangible profit.

Lastly, monitoring and evolving based on engagement metrics ensures that the techniques applied are yielding the desired returns. Vigilance in tracking changes in engagement patterns, testing different strategies, and adapting to the shifting landscape of Facebook enables a constantly optimized approach to monetizing online interactions.

Profit, then, is not merely the result of accidental virality but the outcome of a meticulously engineered tapestry of interactions that uplift both the user experience and the brand's bottom line. Through consistent effort, strategic planning, and a nurturing of relationally rich engagement, profitability on Facebook becomes not just possible, but probable.

CHAPTER 11

YouTube - Views to Value

Embarking on the journey from passive viewer to active creator, one learns that YouTube is more than a platform for entertainment; it's a vibrant marketplace, teeming with opportunities for those who dare to transform views into value. In this chapter, we delve into the intricacies of creating a YouTube channel that resonates with audiences and leaves a lasting impact. We consider the nuances of content that engages and inspires, the types that not only attract eyes but also foster communities. Furthermore, we explore YouTube's monetization policies and the various avenues through which ad revenue can be maximized. Transformative stories from successful YouTubers serve not merely as motivation but as roadmaps that highlight the importance of authenticity, strategic planning, and audience connection in the alchemy of turning visual stories into financial success. Embrace the rhythm of this digital dance—where consistency, creativity, and value intersect to generate a harmonious monetization melody.

Creating a YouTube Channel with Impact

Embarking on the journey of creating a YouTube channel is an adventure that blends creativity with strategy. Beyond the initial excitement, there is a compelling vision that must be honed, one where dynamic content meets a swelling tide of viewers looking to not only be entertained but also informed, inspired, and engaged.

The inception of your channel requires precise thought on the kind of impact you aim to have. Consider what value your channel will offer. Will it teach skills, generate laughter, promote wellness, or share knowledge? Understanding the transformative power of your content is pivotal in carving out a unique space amongst the millions of channels already in existence.

Central to this endeavor is identifying your niche — that specific area where your passion and expertise intersect with the demands of a particular audience. Research intensively to discover gaps in content that you can expertly fill, or find new angles to existing subjects that can captivate an audience.

A channel's branding should not be overlooked. It speaks volumes before the play button is ever clicked. This encompasses your channel name, logo, banner, and overall aesthetic. All of these elements should resonate with your target audience and reflect the essence of your unique selling proposition.

Craft compelling content that not only attracts viewers but retains them. Your videos should be structured with clear narratives or information that is digestible and resonant. Whether it's through storytelling, demonstration, or expressive commentary, ensure that each video has a defined purpose and call-to-action.

The quality of your videos can act as a silent ambassador of your dedication. Invest in good lighting, clear audio, and a decent camera. However, do not let perfection hinder progress; you can start with what you have and improve over time as resources permit.

Consistency in content creation cannot be understated. Plan a content calendar and stick to a regular upload schedule. Viewers appreciate predictability and are more likely to stay engaged with channels that deliver content consistently. This also aids the YouTube algorithm in understanding the cadence of your postings, which can affect your visibility on the platform.

Optimize each video for search by understanding the intricacies of SEO. Use relevant keywords in your titles, descriptions, and tags to increase your discoverability. Remember, YouTube is the second-largest search engine in the world, and optimization is a key player in harnessing its power.

Engagement with your audience goes beyond responding to comments. It involves actively creating a community around your channel. Encourage viewer interaction through calls to action, asking for comments, and perhaps driving discussions on your other social media platforms to foster a deeper connection.

Collaborating with other YouTubers can propel your channel into new stratospheres. It facilitates cross-pollination of ideas and audiences, leading to increased exposure and the potential for impactful partnerships. Network with peers and explore collaboration opportunities that align with your channel's mission.

Analyze your channel's performance regularly through YouTube Analytics. This tool offers a deep dive into the metrics of your videos and overall channel health. Utilize this invaluable data to refine your content strategy, understand your audience better, and make informed decisions that steer your channel's growth.

Remember, sustaining a YouTube channel necessitates resilience. There will be times of slow growth or unexpected challenges. See these as opportunities to learn and evolve, rather than reasons to halt your efforts. Every great channel was once a beginner — consistency and flexibility in approach will set the foundation for long-lasting impact.

Promoting your channel should be proactive and multifaceted. Leverage multiple social media platforms, engage in online communities related to your niche, and perhaps even invest in targeted advertising to increase your channel's visibility and draw in a dedicated viewer base.

Finally, set realistic goals and timelines for your channel's growth. Understand that building a YouTube channel with impact is a progression that entails patience and persistence. Celebrate milestones, no matter how small, and use them as stepping stones towards your larger vision. Your channel is a canvas to not only broadcast content but also to create genuine connections and influence — wield it with intention and unwavering commitment.

As you continue to nurture and develop your YouTube channel, remember that it represents a confluence of effort, strategy, and heart. A channel with impact is not just measured by the number of subscribers but by the change it incites — whether that's through empowering individuals, fostering communities, or simply bringing joy. Forge ahead with clarity and conviction, and let your digital grandeur unfold.

Monetization Policies and Ad Revenue

As we continue to delve into the depths of digital revenue generation, let us steer our focus towards the intricacies of YouTube—a platform that has evolved from a mere video-sharing site to a powerful income-enabler. The monetization policies and ad revenue mechanisms on YouTube form a cornerstone for creators looking to monetize their content. Understanding these policies is not just important; it's imperative for anyone aiming to harness the financial power of this global platform.

YouTube's Partner Program (YPP) is the gateway through which creators can earn money. To be eligible, there are prerequisite conditions such as having a minimum of 1,000 subscribers, accruing at least 4,000 watch hours over the last 12 months, and ensuring adherence to all of YouTube's policies and guidelines. Once these metrics are met, creators can apply to the program and, upon acceptance, start earning from ads shown on their videos.

Ad revenue represents a significant share of YouTube earnings for most creators. Ads can be displayed in several forms—pre-roll, mid-roll, display, and overlay among others. The type of ads utilized and their placement within the content can influence both viewer experience and revenue generation. Creators must straddle the line between monetization and maintaining an enjoyable viewer experience.

YouTube uses a Cost Per Mille (CPM) or Cost Per Click (CPC) model to determine earnings from ads. CPM refers to the amount an advertiser pays for one thousand views or impressions of an advertisement, while CPC is the amount paid for each click on an ad. Navigating these models requires a nuanced approach to content creation where understanding one's audience and their engagement behaviors is key.

It is important to note that the choice of topics and adherence to community guidelines significantly impact monetization. YouTube's algorithm favors advertiser-friendly content, which means videos that feature controversial or explicit material may not be eligible for monetization. A profound understanding of these guidelines ensures creators are not inadvertently limiting their potential earnings.

Another avenue within YouTube's monetization framework is channel memberships, where viewers pay a monthly fee for access to exclusive perks provided by the creator. Such features, including Super Chat and Super Stickers, enable direct monetary contributions from viewers during live streams and offer additional revenue streams, supplementing ad earnings.

For channels with content appealing to younger audience members, such as children's programming, monetization policies are even more stringent due to heightened considerations around child safety and compliance with regulations such as the Children's Online Privacy Protection Act (COPPA). These channels must navigate these additional layers of policy while maximizing their revenue potential.

Creators should also consider the role that seasonality plays in ad revenue. Certain times of the year, like the holiday season, can see a spike in ad spend, while others may experience a lull. Capitalizing on these trends by aligning content release schedules with high-ad-spend periods can lead to increased earnings.

International creators must also take into account YouTube's varying policies across different countries. Tax obligations, for instance, may differ, affecting the net earnings from ad revenue. A forward-looking creator must maintain an updated understanding of international policies to optimize their global earning potential.

Data analytics tools provided by YouTube can guide creators through the labyrinth of monetization. The Analysis tab in

YouTube Studio offers insights into which videos are earning the most revenue, demographic information of viewers, and the performance of different ad types. By sifting through this data, creators can adapt their strategies to amplify ad revenue.

It's worth mentioning that the number of views a video garners is not always directly proportional to the revenue it earns. Metrics such as viewer engagement time, audience demographics, and the advertisers' targeted audiences can significantly influence the earning potential of a piece of content. Creators must aim to optimize these metrics to attract higher-paying advertisements.

Effort should also be invested in cultivating a sustainable, engaged community. Followers who interact regularly and positively with content increase the channel's appeal to advertisers. Community engagement through comments, likes, and shares can signal to YouTube's algorithms that a channel's content is worth promoting to broader audiences, thereby enhancing opportunities for higher ad revenue.

Finally, creators should diversify their revenue sources. While ad revenue is important, relying solely on it can be precarious due to policy changes or shifts in market trends. Integrating merchandise sales, sponsorship deals, and crowdfunding can provide a financial buffer and ensure a steady income flow despite fluctuating ad revenue.

Monetizing content on YouTube through ad revenue is a sophisticated dance of content creation, community engagement, and a deep understanding of the platform's policies. The creators who study the rhythm, learning each step and turn, are the ones who find themselves in harmony with success, transforming their creative expressions into lucrative businesses.

With diligence, perseverance, and astute management, the alliance of content and commerce on YouTube can be a wellspring of financial prosperity. And as we equip ourselves with the knowledge of these monetization policies and strategies to maximize ad revenue, we prepare to take our place among those thriving in this dynamic sphere of digital creation and income generation.

WhatsApp for Wealth - Chat Your Way to Cash

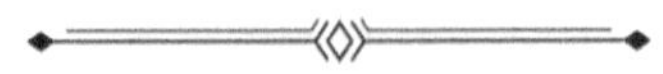

The journey into the digital age invites us to harness the power of connectivity in innovative ways, and WhatsApp emerges as an unlikely yet potent vehicle for economic advancement. Chapter 12 delves into the world of WhatsApp as it transcends the limits of casual messaging to become a thriving marketplace for the astute entrepreneur. Here, we explore how this app, with its simple interfaces and global reach, can be intricately woven into your business strategy to monetize conversations and networks effectively. Whether it's through personalized customer service that nurtures trust, or the strategic utilization of WhatsApp Business to streamline sales and marketing processes, you're on the brink of transforming the way you interact with your clients. This chapter guides you through the art of cultivating a community around your product or service, transforming your contacts list into a dynamic customer base. With the emphasis on actionable tactics, you'll learn to tap into the rich potential that lies within WhatsApp, effortlessly turning exchanges into opportunities and, ultimately, crafting a wealth narrative that is as rewarding as it is profound.

Utilizing WhatsApp for Business and Commerce

Since its inception, WhatsApp has transformed from a mere messaging app into a powerful tool for businesses and entrepreneurs seeking to carve a niche in the digital commerce arena. As we explore the uses of social media and the internet for wealth creation, WhatsApp presents itself as a unique platform where simplicity and widespread adoption converge to offer significant commercial opportunities.

The world has transcended traditional business models, and in this digital epoch, agility and innovation stand at the forefront of commercial success. WhatsApp, with its burgeoning user base, provides businesses a direct communication line to their customers. The WhatsApp Business application, an iteration specifically designed for small and medium-sized businesses, encapsulates features that are not only user-friendly but also highly conducive to fostering customer relationships.

To begin harnessing WhatsApp for business purposes, one must first comprehend the application's core functionalities which include catalog creation, business profiles, and the use of automated messaging. A business profile on WhatsApp serves as your digital business card, succinct but informative, offering your customers insight into what services or goods you offer at a glance.

But the functionalities do not end there. The strategic integration of chatbots and quick replies can significantly augment conversation management, ensuring that your responses to common queries are not only immediate but also consistently accurate. This application of technology to simulate personable interaction with customers can lead to enhanced customer satisfaction and loyalty.

In the realm of business, trust is paramount, and WhatsApp furthers this by providing end-to-end encryption. This built-in security feature guarantees that your business conversations remain confidential, thereby nurturing a sense of security and trust between you and your clientele.

Transitioning from communication to commerce, one of the most powerful features of WhatsApp is the ability to create and share a product catalog. This feature allows businesses to showcase their products in a format that is easy to browse and share. Customers can peruse your offerings, making their selections directly within a chat interface that feels familiar and comfortable, without being redirected to external websites or applications.

Moreover, timing is crucial in business, and WhatsApp Business can help streamline the transaction process. Features like sending invoices, order summaries, or even payment requests directly in the chat ensure businesses capitalize on the momentum of customer interest.

Another concept worth emphasizing is the utilization of WhatsApp status updates to engage with customers. Much like stories on other social platforms, these ephemeral snippets can be leveraged to announce new products, share testimonials, or offer time-limited promotions, thereby keeping your audience informed and engaged in real-time.

However, to truly scale your WhatsApp-driven business, you need to cultivate a growth-focused strategy. This involves segmenting your audience using labels, personalizing communication to cater to different customer groups effectively, and analyzing the 'WhatsApp for Business' analytics to fine-tune your approach based on customer interaction data.

As we pivot towards the importance of feedback, encouraging customers to contact you on WhatsApp for after-sales service can enhance customer experience and provide invaluable insights into customer satisfaction. This establishes a feedback loop that not only aids in improving your product or service but also reinforces the customer's importance to your business.

To expand your reach, integrating your WhatsApp Business number onto different digital platforms such as your website, email signatures, or social media profiles is crucial. It creates a cohesive omnichannel experience for your customers, making it easy for them to connect with you on their preferred platform.

A forward-thinking entrepreneur also considers the power of collaborations and partnerships. Engaging with influencers or other businesses in your niche can lead to cross-promotions or co-marketing efforts on WhatsApp, tapping into new audiences and amplifying your brand's visibility.

Moreover, as you chart your journey through the digital commerce world on WhatsApp, ensure you're mindful of local regulations and WhatsApp's business policies. Adhering to guidelines not only prevents you from potential legal pitfalls but also maintains the integrity and reputation of your business.

Lastly, in this pursuit of success through WhatsApp, it's crucial to maintain a balance between automation and genuine human connection. While automated messages can serve efficiency, they can't replace the warmth of human interaction which is essential when building lasting relationships with customers.

In conclusion, WhatsApp stands as a testament to the evolution of business in the digital age. With an emphasis on simplicity, security, and personal engagement, WhatsApp for Business manifests as an opportune platform for commerce that can lead to a thriving digital business. Its features, when leveraged with creativity and strategic planning, can open doors to a global marketplace right from the palm of your hand.

Growing Your Audience and Customer Base lies at the core of capitalizing on the ubiquitous nature of platforms such as WhatsApp for business endeavors. The path to amplification of reach and subsequently bolstering your customer base is neither instantaneous nor accidental. It is the upshot of measured strategies, unwavering commitment, and keen insight into audience behavior.

In this segment, you will find a roadmap that aligns with the essence of digital communication – attracting and retaining an audience in a space where attention is fragmented but opportunities abundant. A well-curated audience serves as the bedrock of any thriving online venture. To commence this journey, one must possess the paramount ability to listen. Through active listening, you understand customer needs, preferences, and feedback, which are indispensable for shaping your offerings and messaging.

Understanding your audience demands a deep dive into analytics. Analytical tools intrinsic to WhatsApp Business and similar platforms yield invaluable data that highlight the psychographics and behaviors of your customer base. Use this data as a nautical chart, navigating through the currents of consumer trends and patterns, enabling you to make informed decisions that resonate with your customers.

Content creation, undeniably, is your beacon. It has to be compelling, valuable, and most importantly, consistent. Content that solves problems or adds value in some form helps in establishing trust, which is vital for audience growth. This trust turns viewers into followers, followers into customers, and customers into loyal ambassadors for your brand.

Interaction must never be undervalued. Engage actively with your contacts through personalized messages and swift responses. Build relationships through engagement, solidifying your presence in their minds as more than a distant entity – but as a reliable, empathetic partner in addressing their needs and aspirations.

Enhance your visibility by exploiting the unique features of WhatsApp, such as Group Chats and Broadcast Lists, to disseminate information effectively. Keeping your audience informed and updated is not a mere courtesy; it is a strategic method of ensuring your brand stays prevalent in discussions.

Collaborations and partnerships can be a powerful tool for audience expansion. Align with individuals or entities that share a complementary vision or customer base. This form of synergy has the potential to introduce your narrative to a broader and diverse audience, fostering growth through the shared value.

Promotions and incentives are a compelling way to foster audience growth. Exclusive deals and special offers for your community can motivate customers to not only engage with your brand but also to spread word-of-mouth recommendations, which are golden in an era where peer opinions are highly revered.

Education and empowerment through workshops, webinars, and live sessions add an additional layer of engagement. When you equip your audience with knowledge and skills, you inadvertently empower them to make decisions that could advantageously incorporate your services or products into their lives or businesses.

As technological advancements rapidly evolve, so should your strategies. Being adaptive to change and receptive to new tools and features ensures that you remain competitive and relevant. Continuously seek out new and innovative ways to connect and provide value to your audience.

Inclusivity should be at the heart of all your undertakings – ensure that your content and interactions span across demographics, respecting and appealing to a global audience. In a cyberspace characterized by diversity, inclusivity can be a substantial differentiator.

Security and trust cannot be overemphasized. Ensure that your operations on WhatsApp and other digital channels are not only compliant with data protection laws but also transparent in how they handle customer information. Privacy assurance significantly boosts customer confidence.

Feedback is a powerful growth accelerant. Encourage it, act on it, and show your customers that their voice shapes your business. This openness not only improves your offerings but also deepens customer relationships, as they regard their input as a component of your success.

Finally, do not chase numbers blindly. A large but disengaged audience serves no purpose. Focus on cultivating a community that is engaged, interested, and active. Quality trumps quantity when it comes to building a steadfast and profitable audience.

In conclusion, audience and customer base growth is a multifaceted endeavor that commands a thoughtful blend of analytics, creativity, interaction, and adaptation. By valuing each customer's journey with your brand, you not only increase your audience size but also enhance the quality of engagement, setting the stage for sustained business success in the vibrant, ever-expanding digital marketplace.

CHAPTER 13

Internet Entrepreneurship - Strategies for Online Business Success

As we pivot from the personalized niches and platforms discussed in prior chapters, it's time to cast the net wider and truly embrace the scope of *Internet Entrepreneurship*. Within this sphere, your business acumen and innovative spirit converge to unlock new avenues for generating income. You'll uncover the cornerstones of successful e-commerce—where products meet their audience with the click of a button. Furthermore, you'll explore the lucrative world of affiliate marketing, where strategic partnerships and passive revenue streams can flourish. It's a chapter for those ready to commit, to construct burgeoning enterprises that stand resilient in the ever-shifting sands of the internet. Empower yourself with proven strategies that harness today's technology, using it as a bastion for success in a competitive online marketplace. Navigate these digital waters with the savvy of an expert and the vision of a pioneer, charging forward to meet your entrepreneurial destiny.

E-commerce Essentials

In the vast expanse of the digital marketplace, e-commerce stands as a beacon of opportunity for those who choose to navigate its waters with purpose and determination. Engaging in e-commerce involves more than setting up a virtual storefront; it requires a foundational understanding of certain key elements to thrive in an online business landscape. This section delves into the essentials of e-commerce and the pivotal aspects that, when mastered, can transform your digital endeavors into prosperous ventures.

The bedrock of effective e-commerce is your website, your portal to global markets. The importance of a user-friendly, responsive design cannot be overstated. First impressions matter greatly in the digital realm. Your website should embody simplicity, clarity, and a transparent user journey. Ensure your web design is optimized for various devices, as a significant portion of consumers access online shopping through mobile platforms.

At the core of e-commerce is your product selection. This crucial element determines not only the direction of your business but also your target market. Identifying products that resonate with consumers, align with your brand values, and stand out in a crowded online space is a strategic imperative. Consistency in product quality and a unique selling proposition (USP) can elevate your offerings above the competition.

Integral to the success of an e-commerce business is a seamless transaction process. Payment gateways are the conduits through which trust is established with your customers. Choose providers that offer security, reliability, and a range of payment options to accommodate buyer preferences. Implementing the latest in encryption and security protocols cultivates a sense of safety, encouraging repeat transactions.

Logistics, while often operating behind the scenes, play a vital role in customer satisfaction. Efficient inventory management, reliable order fulfillment, and timely shipping arrangements are the pillars of operational excellence. Your ability to deliver products promptly and accurately reflects on your brand's reputation, reinforcing customer trust and loyalty.

In this digital era, personalization in e-commerce is not just an option but an expectation. Leverage data analytics to understand customer preferences, customize the shopping experience, and offer tailored recommendations. A personalized touch can create an emotional connection with your customers, engendering a sense of belonging to your brand community.

Customer service in the digital space becomes a complex tapestry that intertwines technology and human empathy. Setting up robust customer support systems, including chatbots for immediate assistance and accessible human support for complex issues, ensures that customer inquiries are handled with care and efficiency.

Marketing strategies for e-commerce must be agile, innovative, and data-driven. Incorporating search engine optimization (SEO), social media marketing, email campaigns, and influencer partnerships can drive traffic and conversions. Remember, your marketing efforts should echo the voice of your brand and speak directly to the hearts and needs of your target audience.

With potential cyber threats lurking, cybersecurity should be a paramount concern for any e-commerce entrepreneur. Regularly update your systems, conduct security audits, and be vigilant about protecting customer data. Customers entrust you with their personal and financial information; safeguarding it is both ethical and essential for your business's sustainability.

Another cornerstone of e-commerce success is scalability. Your digital infrastructure needs to be capable of growing and adapting to increased demand. Cloud-based solutions offer flexibility and scalability to adjust resources in real-time, enabling you to manage spikes in website traffic and sales volume without compromising performance.

Understand the legalities that govern e-commerce operations, including tax obligations, intellectual property rights, and consumer protection laws. Adhering to regulations not only keeps your business compliant but also cements your reputation as a trustworthy merchant.

A robust return policy and money-back guarantees can diminish purchase hesitation and bolster consumer confidence. Clearly state your return policy, make it fair and visible, and handle returns and exchanges with professionalism. Such policies display a commitment to customer satisfaction and can be a decisive factor in driving sales.

Collecting and utilizing customer feedback propels a culture of continuous improvement. Encourage reviews, engage with customer feedback, and be receptive to constructive criticism. Utilizing this intel helps refine your offerings and service, aligning them more closely with customer expectations.

Explore the integration of emerging technologies, such as augmented reality (AR) and artificial intelligence (AI), to enhance the online shopping experience. AR can offer customers a virtual try-before-you-buy experience, and AI can personalize shopping in ways previously unimaginable, fostering deep customer engagement.

To maintain a competitive edge in e-commerce, stay informed about current trends and industry updates. Attend workshops, webinars, and seek the wisdom of mentors. Learning is an ongoing process, and staying ahead of the curve is imperative.

Finally, nurture a community around your e-commerce brand. Facilitate conversations and build relationships with your customers through social media, forums, and events. A strong, involved community can become both your brand champions and a source of invaluable market insight.

These e-commerce essentials form the compass by which to chart your course in the digital trade winds. As you apply these principles with consistency and vision, you'll find that your online enterprise is not just a transactional endeavor but a transformative journey that connects you to a world of individuals seeking value, convenience, and engagement in every click and tap. Embrace the challenge, for in doing so, you unlock the door to boundless opportunity and digital prosperity.

Affiliate Marketing and Passive Income

The pathway to financial freedom is paved with a myriad of strategies and opportunities. Among them, affiliate marketing stands out as a beacon for those seeking to generate revenue in the digital world. Enabling you to earn while you sleep, it's the epitome of passive income—a pot of gold that doesn't require constant labor to maintain its glisten. As we explore this avenue, remember that the digital space is vast, and within it lies the potential to craft an income stream that aligns with your passions and expertise.

At its core, affiliate marketing is a performance-based marketing strategy in which an online retailer rewards you—a partner or affiliate—for each visitor or customer brought about by your marketing efforts. You are, in essence, a bridge between the consumer and the product. This creates a unique opportunity for you to weave products or services seamlessly into your digital content, serving both the needs of your audience and the ambitions of your financial goals.

To begin, select an affiliate program that resonates with your personal brand and audience. Be patient in this process, for the most lucrative partnerships are those that stand the test of authenticity. Your audience trusts your voice, and it's imperative to honor that trust by choosing to affiliate with products and services you genuinely endorse.

Once you have chosen a program, the real work begins—creating content that adds value to your audience while incorporating your affiliate offerings. Whether it's through writing insightful blog posts, recording compelling videos, or crafting engaging social media posts, your content should serve as both a platform for discussion and a catalyst for action.

Keywords and SEO play a pivotal role in ensuring that your content reaches its intended audience. Your affiliate content must be discoverable, and thus understanding search engine optimization is key. Optimize your content to ensure it ranks well, thereby increasing visibility and, ultimately, the likelihood of click-throughs and conversions.

With content published, the passive nature of affiliate marketing begins to shine. Each piece of content can act as a perennial source of income, bearing fruit long after it's been created. It's essential, however, to maintain and update your content to keep it relevant in the ever-evolving chasm of the internet.

Email marketing is yet another potent tool in the affiliate marketer's kit. By building a robust email list and sending out strategically timed and well-crafted messages, you can consistently drive your subscribers back to your content and affiliate offers. This isn't merely about pushing products—it's about offering solutions and experiences that align with the needs and desires of your audience.

Diversification is prudent in any financial venture, and affiliate marketing is no different. Do not tether your fate to a single affiliate program or product. Expand your portfolio, align with multiple programs, and insulate yourself against the volatile nature of the digital marketplace. The most successful affiliate marketers are those that serve a variety of niches and utilize numerous channels to spread their influence.

Tracking and analyzing performance is crucial. Employ analytics tools to measure the effectiveness of your affiliate campaigns. Understand what content performs best, what products resonate most with your audience, and replicate these results. Adaptability is key; pivot and evolve as metrics guide your decisions.

Risk is an innate aspect of all endeavors, affiliate marketing included. Be prepared to face the fact that not all efforts will translate to success. However, don't succumb to discouragement; it is in the nature of risk that lessons are learned and strategies are honed. Embrace every stumble as a stepping stone to a more refined approach.

One must also consider the legalities that come with affiliate marketing. Be transparent in your dealings—disclose your affiliate relationships to your audience. Integrity must be the foundation of all your online transactions; it is the bedrock upon which long-term success is built.

Venturing into affiliate marketing requires fortitude, for the sphere is competitive and ever-changing. It awaits those with the discipline to learn, the creativity to innovate, and the patience to nurture growth over time. The rewards, however, can be substantial, providing not just a supplementary source of income but often replacing traditional employment altogether.

In marrying affiliate marketing with the right mindset and strategies, you open doors to an empowering mode of income. It is a testament to the notion that with the right blend of technology and entrepreneurship, financial independence is no longer just a dream—it is an achievable reality.

As we move into the later chapters of our exploration, it's important to build on these principles of affiliate marketing and passive income. Learning to capitalize on the opportunities the digital domain presents will be a journey of both dedication and discovery—a journey that promises to reshape notions of income and employment.

Passive income, in particular, grants the gift of time, allowing you to pursue further endeavors, passions, or learning, all while your established income channels continue to contribute to your financial well-being. Embrace these opportunities and let them guide you toward a future where your financial security is defined not by how many hours you trade for dollars but by the intelligent systems you put in place to work on your behalf.

CHAPTER 14

Early Bird or Night Owl - Act Now, It's Never Too Early or Late

In the symphony of digital entrepreneurship, success isn't reserved for those who rise at dawn or burn the midnight oil; rather, it's the immediacy of one's action that orchestrates enduring success. Time, in its relentless march, cares not for our hesitations. As we dive into this chapter, we'll embrace the idea that the right moment is a myth—a construct that can no longer bind us. Whether you're starting your journey amidst the golden hues of morning or under the cloak of night, the digital world operates on a ceaseless cycle, accessible to all who yearn to tap into its boundless potential. We've navigated realms from Instagram to WhatsApp, unearthing strategies for materializing wealth. Now, we stand at the precipice of decision, understanding that the inertia of inaction is the greatest adversary to our digital dreams. Let us dismiss the notion of ill-timed ventures; for the opportunities that buzz through the cyberspace are indifferent to the clock's hands, eagerly awaiting those with the tenacity to seize them. In this chapter, the inspirational narratives of those who defied the odds at diverse junctures of life affirm that indeed, in the journey toward digital prosperity, it's never too early or late to flourish. So let us summon the courage to embark on this quest now, emboldened by the knowledge that our actions today are the architects of our future triumphs.

Why Timing Matters Less Than You Think

In our journey through the captivating world of digital income, we've explored the breadth of opportunities that lie in wait. Yet, there's a pervasive myth that can't be ignored: the belief that timing is the key to unlocking the gates of success. While it's true that being early or late to market can have advantages and disadvantages, it's not the end-all of your entrepreneurial endeavors.

Consider the rhythms of the internet – it's always awake, always engaging, and always evolving. The hallmark of this digital space is its ability to adapt and its capacity to welcome new innovators at any stage. There is no perfect moment that one must wait for; time in the digital realm flows without prejudice towards early birds or night owls. The initiative, then, beats timing. Your decision to act is ultimately more significant than the ticking clock.

Indeed, the stars in the digital sky have aligned for continuous harvesting. Unlike the time-sensitive nature of traditional markets, the internet operates on a 24/7 basis, allowing accessibility at all hours. This means that regardless of when you jump in, there is an audience ready to engage, a customer waiting to be captivated, or a follower eager to listen.

Furthermore, the stories of those who found fame and fortune on the internet rarely fixate on the exact moment they began. Instead, they hinge on persistent efforts, strategic pivots, and contributions to their respective communities. The date of their digital debut fades into the background as their journey takes center stage. These narratives encourage us that our own success isn't tied to a particular timestamp.

The diversity of platforms also bears testament to this timeless approach. Whether your channel of choice is Instagram, Facebook, YouTube, WhatsApp, or an emerging platform, each is designed with the acuity to serve up content to the right person at the right time, using algorithms that favor relevance over recency.

Consider the liberation this brings: the perfectionist's paralysis, the constant gaze upon the ideal conditions – they fall away, yielding to action and growth. Every moment becomes opportune, and every initiative is as fresh as its execution. It's not when you start that sets you apart, but how you continue to develop and maintain your digital presence.

In discussing the irrelevance of timing, we should also acknowledge the constancy of change online. What works today may evolve tomorrow, and what's trending now may be forgotten next week. Yet, if you're ingrained in the process, consistently learning and adapting, you won't be left behind – you'll be a part of the evolution. This is essential in areas like e-commerce and affiliate marketing, where agility trumps all.

Your digital income strategy is akin to planting a seed. It may not be the first in the ground, but with the right care and nurturing, it can grow to match or surpass those that were. This nurturing involves optimizing your content, engaging with your community, and providing value that resonates with your audience.

It's imperative to realize that the digital landscape is forgiving for latecomers. Strategy, diligence, and creativity fill the void left by less-than-perfect timing. You might stumble upon an untapped niche or a new demand that others, fixated on the clock, have overlooked.

As we acknowledge the lesser significance of timing, we wrap ourselves in the wisdom that every second is ripe with potential for action. Today's platforms have blurred the lines between day and night, have made moot the concept of 'too soon' or 'too late,' and instead reward the bold who choose to embark regardless of the hour.

Don't let the myth of timing deter you. Instead, step boldly into the world of social media, the internet, and cyberspace to carve your path and forge your success. It's your consistent effort and adaptability that will make your digital income endeavors fruitful. Act now, and let's create the future, a future unbounded by the confines of a clock.

Embrace this liberating perspective — time doesn't dictate your potential for success; your actions do. Let's celebrate the beauty of this truth as we move forward in this digital epoch, unfettered by the ticking hands of time.

Success Stories: Late Bloomers in the Digital Realm

In the pursuit of digital prosperity, many fear that the ship has sailed without them, that it's too late to claim a space in the vast expanse of the internet. Yet, there are inspiring narratives that challenge this notion, tales of individuals who rose to prominence not in the dawn but in the twilight of their careers. These late bloomers discovered the boundless opportunities that technology offers, irrespective of the hour. Their stories are testaments to the reality that timing is important, but resolve and adaptability are paramount.

Consider Susan, who after decades of traditional employment, found herself at odds with a rapidly changing professional landscape. She dipped her toes into the digital pool and soon found herself swimming with the tide, using her prowess in knitting to create an online craft business. Her venture, now a celebrated blog featuring tutorials and a marketplace, is frequented by thousands of enthusiasts. Susan's story speaks volumes; it reveals that the digital world values skill and passion over age or the speed at which one embraces technology.

Then there is Roberto, a retired military officer who turned his disciplined lifestyle into a coaching business. He adapted his life's lessons into courses and webinars, eventually building a community around leadership and personal development. Roberto's story is invigorating, for it shows how the digital realm respects no background, only the value one can provide to others through their experiences and knowledge. His success in the digital space bloomed late but swiftly, as if making up for lost time.

There's also the story of Grace, a homemaker whose children had flown the nest. Finding a new chapter in life, she took to the digital stage, sharing her culinary prowess. What began as a modest food blog burgeoned into a multimedia empire, with videos, e-books, and even her line of cookware. Grace's voyage in the cyber sea was not a tale of a ship sailing smoothly; it was one of weathering storms with tenacity, proving that it's not the early start but the steady journey that counts.

These narratives are not anomalies; they are beacons for anyone who feels that the digital sunset is upon them. They tell us that it is not merely the youthful or the tech-native who can excel in this realm. What's required is a willingness to learn, adapt, and apply one's strengths to the opportunities that abound in cyberspace. Achievement isn't exclusive to those who grew up with the internet; it waits eagerly for anyone willing to reach out and grasp it. Age, then, is merely a number, not a barrier.

Fostering digital acumen later in life often comes with advantages: a wealth of experience, a network of contacts, and a maturity of thought. Late bloomers tend to be strategic in their online ventures, more deliberate in their actions, knowing well that every click, every post, and every interaction is a seed planted for future harvest.

Late bloomers also bring with them a unique voice, one seasoned by experience. Unlike those who may echo the digital echo chamber, they often stand out with their unique perspectives. The digital audience is vast and diverse, craving authenticity and substance, which the late bloomer can provide in abundance. Their stories resonate with a wide base, for they carry with them the weight of lived wisdom and genuine insight.

Moreover, the digital platform celebrates the diversity of content and ideas, a realm where niche passions can find a global audience. The retiree with a zeal for historic restoration, the mother who champions sustainability, the veteran with insights on resilience—all find their tribes within the digital expanse. This democratization of reach means that it's never too late for the late starter to find their space and thrive within it.

A crucial element in these success stories is the recognition that the journey will be one of learning and growth. For each late bloomer who thrives, there have been moments of doubt, of fumbling with unfamiliar tools, of grappling with the new language of digital engagement. But with each uncertainty navigated, each skill mastered, they become not only participants in the digital economy but shapers of it.

Take the example of Martin, whose career in accounting gave him precision but little creative outlet. At the urging of his grandchildren, he started a finance blog, combining fiscal advice with personal anecdotes. His ability to demystify complex economic principles has earned him a dedicated following and speaking engagements. Martin's story is insightful: it teaches that traditional skills can find a new lease on life within the digital economy.

The late bloomer's success is also predicated on the embrace of community and collaboration. In a realm where information transfer is lightning-fast, learning from peers, building relationships with followers, and engaging with mentors can significantly accelerate one's progress. The success of Ellie, who created a wellness community, stands as evidence. Nurtured by her empathy and encouraged by collaborative ventures, her brand flourished as a haven for holistic health aficionados.

Each success story also underscores the importance of adaptability and the willingness to embrace change. Digitization has a transformative effect, both on industries and individuals. Learning new software, understanding the algorithmic pulse of social platforms, and pivoting strategies in response to online trends aren't just tasks; they are the stepping stones to digital viability and longevity.

Consider also the importance of resilience in this context. Each digital entrepreneur will face setbacks, algorithm changes, and perhaps even public criticism. Yet, the late bloomer is often well-equipped to handle adversity, armed with the fortitude forged from a lifetime of varied experiences. It is this resilience that not only endears them to their audience but also ensures their continuity in an ever-evolving digital marketplace.

In closing, the late bloomers in the digital realm are nothing short of inspirational icons. They prove that the digital domain doesn't exclusively belong to those who started their journey at its genesis. It is an inclusive space, waiting with bated breath for the next unique idea, the next untold story, the next unexpected educator. These champions of the cyber world have demonstrated that the digital revolution isn't reserved for any particular age group or demographic—it's an equal opportunity realm, ripe for the taking.

As we explore these remarkable journeys, we're reminded of the fundamental truth that our digital economy thrives on diversity, on the unique contributions of its participants, regardless of when they choose to join the dance. Whether you're considering your first foray into the digital realm or you're already wading through its waters, let these stories be a beacon of hope, a guide, but most importantly, a testament to the power of starting where you are, using what you have, and doing what you can. The digital sphere awaits your narrative—may it be as enriching and as inspiring as those who've tread the path before you.

CHAPTER 15

Your Digital Dollar Future - Scaling and Maintaining Your Online Income

Once you've fine-tuned the art of earning online and carved out your virtual niche, the natural progression leads us to expansion and stabilization. Mastering sustained growth in your digital ventures is akin to tending a fruitful, burgeoning garden. It requires consistent nurturing, adaptability, and shrewd pruning to flourish. This chapter delves into sophisticated strategies that anchor your online earnings, turning sporadic success into a robust, thriving financial ecosystem. Harness a mindset of continuous innovation to keep pace with the ever-changing digital landscape; safeguarding your assets against volatility demands a keen eye on trend forecasts and algorithm updates. Balancing these elements with a focus on scalability empowers you to broaden your influence and income, while maintaining a steadfast grip on the integrity and authenticity of your brand. As your online income grows, you'll not only relish the fruits of your labor, but also be able to reinvest in your most valuable asset: yourself, ensuring the perpetuity of success in your digital dollar future.

Long-Term Digital Wealth Strategies

In the quest to achieve enduring digital wealth, longevity and sustainability must be at the forefront of our thinking. In the evolving landscape of the digital economy, one cannot merely rest on short-term gains and tactics. Instead, a vision that extends beyond the present, forging into the future, is required. Crafting long-term digital wealth strategies is akin to sowing seeds with intent, nurturing them through seasons, and watching them bear fruit over many harvests.

Laying the foundation of long-term wealth begins with diversification. Diversifying income streams across various digital platforms ensures that you are not heavily reliant on a single source, which may fluctuate or even become obsolete over time. This might involve balancing active ventures on platforms like Instagram and YouTube with passive income strategies such as affiliate marketing or e-commerce.

Investment in learning and personal development is another critical component. As the digital domain perpetually advances, continuous education keeps you updated with the latest trends, tools, and strategies. It can transform the way you engage with technology and help you adapt to changes as they arise. Subscribing to industry publications, participating in relevant webinars, and attending conferences are all valuable means of staying informed and skillful.

Building a brand that resonates with authenticity and value can anchor one's presence in the digital space. Your brand is a reflection of your identity online. As such, it should communicate a clear, consistent message across all platforms. A strong brand not only gains recognition but also engenders trust and loyalty among your audience, which is the cornerstone of sustained success.

Strategic partnerships and collaborations can amplify your reach and add to the robustness of your digital empire. By uniting with others in your niche or industry, you can leverage mutual strengths, share audiences, and create joint ventures that are more potent than individual efforts. These collaborations should be selective, intentional, and aligned with your brand's values and long-term objectives.

Reinvestment in one's digital endeavors is an often overlooked strategy. Profits garnered from digital platforms should not just be treated as earnings but as capital. A percentage should consistently be reinvested into the business to fuel growth, whether through advertising, new technology, or hiring talent to expand your capabilities.

Maximizing automation and technology can result in exponential growth. Implementing systems that automate repetitive tasks, such as email responses or social media posting, frees up time to focus on strategy and expansion. The utilization of data analytics tools can provide insights into your audience and operational efficiencies, driving more informed decisions.

Avoiding common pitfalls is essential to ensuring longevity. This includes not falling for get-rich-quick traps, spreading oneself too thin across platforms, or violating platform policies which could result in bans or penalties. Deepening your understanding of the legal and ethical implications of online business practices protects your income streams and reputation.

Immersion in new and emerging platforms might be daunting, yet it is a necessary risk for enduring success. Early adoption of fresh technologies or platforms can position you as a pioneer, giving you the advantage of settling in and carving out your space before the market becomes saturated.

Embracing the flexibility of the digital landscape means being open to pivoting when necessary. What works today may not work tomorrow. As your audience evolves, so too should your strategies and content. Regularly evaluating and adjusting your approach ensures that your digital business remains relevant and progressive.

Creating a community rather than just an audience can lead to sustainable growth. Engage with your followers by fostering meaningful interactions and building a network of support. This community becomes a bedrock – not only do they consume your content and products but also advocate on your behalf.

Intellectual property protection cannot be ignored in the digital arena. Ensuring that your ideas, content, and creations are legally safeguarded fortifies your business against theft and plagiarism. This involves understanding copyright laws, trademarks, and patents relevant to your work.

Prioritizing user experience on all your platforms can solidify your digital presence. In the fast-paced digital world, consumers have a plethora of options, and a poor user experience can drive them away quickly. To maintain and grow your audience, ensure that your websites, apps, and social media are intuitive, accessible, and enjoyable to interact with.

Financial planning and management form the backbone of long-term wealth. Employ sound fiscal practices by budgeting, tracking income and expenses, and planning for taxes. Being financially disciplined not only safeguards your current earnings but secures your future within the digital domain.

Finally, embracing a mindset that is both visionary and adaptable propels you to new heights. Your mindset determines your approach to challenges, your resilience in face of change, and your willingness to innovate. Cultivating such a mindset is a catalyst for sustainable digital wealth.

In conclusion, the strategies for long-term digital wealth are numerous and interconnected. They require both the heart of an artist and the mind of an entrepreneur. By diversifying, being agile, maintaining authenticity, and keeping the future in focus, you mark your path with stepping stones that lead to not only financial prosperity but a legacy in the digital world. The path won't always be straightforward, but as you build and optimize these strategies, your digital wealth can and will flourish over time.

Conclusion

I am convinced that our journey thus far in exploiting this topic has been extremely eye opening, motivating and instructional. The step-by-step approach provided in this book remains a well proven concept that has the potential of raining down dollars from our everyday digital experiences.

It is expected that readers will take heed and meticulously follow through with all the strategies laid out in the various chapters and sections of this masterpiece.

I have poured my heart, skills and knowledge into this book because I believe that you too can join the camp of millions across the globe who continues to make a fortune from the internet via our everyday interactions and partnership in the democratized social media and internet space.

The opportunities is for all and across all social and economic strata, so you have no excuse to fail, rather an opportunity to take those actions as laid out in the book and make history too.

I wish you the very best.